Donkeys' Y

Michael Frayn was born in London in 1933 and read
Russian, French and Moral Sciences (Philosophy) at
Emmanuel College, Cambridge. He began his career as a
journalist on the *Manchester Guardian* and the *Observer*. His
award-winning plays include *Alphabetical Order*, *Make and Break*
and *Noises Off*, all of which received Best Comedy of the Year
awards, while *Benefactors* was named Best Play of the Year.
Other recent works include *Democracy*, the fourteenth of his
plays, and *Copenhagen*, both winners of numerous awards
including the *Evening Standard* Best Play award and (for *Copenhagen*
in New York) a Tony award. He has translated Chekhov's last
four plays, dramatised a selection of his one-act plays and
short stories under the title *The Sneeze*, and adapted his first,
untitled play, as *Wild Honey*. His novels include *Towards the End
of the Morning* (in the USA, *Against Entropy*), *The Trick of It*, *A
Landing on the Sun*, *Headlong* and *Spies*. Methuen has published
two selections of his columns, *The Original Michael Frayn* and
The Additional Michael Frayn. He is married to the biographer
and critic Claire Tomalin.

Michael Frayn

Donkeys' Years

Methuen Drama

Published by A&C Black Limited 2006

3 5 7 9 10 8 6 4 2

This edition first published in 2006 by
A&C Black Publishers Limited
38 Soho Square
London W1D 3HB

Copyright © 1977, 2006 by Michael Frayn

The text of this edition incorporates revisions
from the 2006 stage production

Michael Frayn has asserted his rights under the Copyright,
Designs and Patents Act, 1988, to be identified
as the author of this work

A CIP catalogue record for this book is available from the British Library

ISBN 978 0 413 77622 8

Typeset by Country Setting, Kingsdown, Kent
Printed and bound in Great Britain by
MPG Books Ltd, Bodmin, Cornwall

Donkeys' Years was first presented by Michael Codron at the Globe Theatre, London, on 15 July 1976. The production was directed by Michael Rudman, and designed by Alan Tagg. The cast was listed in the programme under the heading:

COLLEGE NOTES

Mr S. Birkett   A. J. Brown
Head Porter, completes fifty years' service
with the College this October

C. D. P. B. Headingley, M.A., M.P.   Peter Barkworth
Parliamentary Under-Secretary of State at
the Department of Education and Science

D. J. Buckle, M.B., M.R.C.S.   Peter Jeffrey
Assistant Chief Surgeon in the Depart-
ment of Urology, Royal Wessex Hospital,
Southampton

K. Snell, M.A.   Andrew Robertson
Engaged in research in parasitology at
British Alkalis (Pharmaceutical Division),
Rotherham

A. V. Quine, B.A.   Julian Curry
Now in the grade of Assistant Secretary at
the Department of Education and Science

The Rev. R. D. Sainsbury, M.A.   Harold Innocent
Curate-in-Charge of St Columba's, Small
Heath, Birmingham

N. O. P. Tate, M.A.   Jeffrey Wickham
Has recently published *The Complete Home
Encyclopaedia of Japanese Flower Arrangement*
and *A Boys' and Girls' Guide to Overseas
Development*

W. R. Taylor, M.A., Ph.D.
Research Fellow and College Lecturer in English, has published *Mythopoeic Structures in the Metonymy of Two Jacobean Children's Rhymes* (*Revue des Études Sémiologiques, Toulouse*)

John Harding

Lady Driver, M.A.
The Master's wife (formerly Rosemary Gilbert), has been appointed a member of the Royal Commission on Obesity

Penelope Keith

Donkeys' Years was revived in its present form by Sonia Friedman Productions, Tulbart Productions, Michael Linnet, Lee Menzies, TEG Productions and Boyett/Ostar Productions at the Comedy Theatre, London, on 27 April 2006. The cast was as follows:

Mr S. Birkett	Edward Petherbridge
C. D. P. B. Headingley, M.A., M.P.	David Haig
D. J. Buckle, M.B., M.R.C.S.	Michael Simkins
K. Snell, M.A.	Mark Addy
A. V. Quine, B.A.	James Dreyfus
The Rev. R. D. Sainsbury, M.A.	Michael Fitzgerald
N. O. P. Tate, M.A.	Jonathan Coy
W. R. Taylor, M.A., Ph.D.	Chris Moran
Lady Driver, M.A.	Samantha Bond

Directed by Jeremy Sams
Designed by Peter McKintosh
Lighting design by Howard Harrison
Sound design by John Leonard

Donkeys' Years

Characters

Birkett
Headingley
Buckle
Snell
Quine
Sainsbury
Tate
Taylor
Lady Driver
Various **Old Members**

Act One

Scene One

One of the smaller courts, in one of the lesser colleges, at one of the older universities.

It's glimpsed at first through the open gate in the front wall of the college. The wall goes out to reveal the whole of the court, with entrances to other courts left and right, and upstage to G staircase.

Birkett *and* **Headingley** *enter left.* **Birkett**, *the Head Porter, is a spry, precise man in his sixties, who, like a head waiter, expresses his air of command as a mannered deference. He is wearing black jacket, striped trousers and bowler hat, and is carrying a clipboard.* **Headingley**, *a successful public man in his mid-forties, is carrying a weekend bag.*

Birkett This way, Mr Headingley, sir, if you please. I've put you in G2. Your old rooms, Mr Headingley, sir.

Headingley Look at the old place!

Birkett Doesn't change very much, does it, sir?

Headingley Doesn't change at all, Mr Birkett. The mulberry tree in the Fellows' Garden . . . King Henry . . . The smell of the river . . . And that Victorian bath-house . . .

Birkett No, they all say the same thing when they come back. 'The old place doesn't change very much, Mr Birkett,' they say. We've our new block down by the river, of course. We've had one or two sit-ins. They've painted King Henry red a few times. But there we are. That's the world we live in. And that's one thing you could say for the gentlemen of your generation. They wouldn't have dreamed of defacing the college. Not when they were sober. That's the difference, you see. Never mind, we always knew you'd do well for us.

Headingley Snakes and ladders, Mr Birkett. Snake next move, for all I know.

Birkett Anyway, we've certainly picked the right day for it.

Headingley   We certainly have, Mr Birkett.

Birkett   We can't complain about the weather today. Come along then, Mr Headingley, sir. You mustn't hold me up, you know. Because they're all coming tonight. Mr Sims, Mr Buckle, Mr Rogers – all your year. I'll tell you one thing, though. The College rowing has never been the same since you went down.

Headingley   I'm not completely forgotten, then, Mr Birkett?

Birkett   Not forgotten by any means, Mr Headingley, sir. Climbing in and out at all hours.

Headingley   Surely not.

Birkett   Yes, indeed, Mr Headingley, sir. Ladies in till breakfast more than once.

Headingley   Never.

Birkett   Oh yes. We don't miss much, Mr Headingley, sir – but we do miss you. Sherry at seven-thirty, Mr Headingley. Dinner at eight. And you haven't forgotten the step, have you, Mr Headingley, sir?

Headingley   I haven't forgotten anything, Mr Birkett. It's curious. I feel as if I'd never been away.

Birkett   That's what they all say, Mr Headingley.

Headingley   In fact I feel rather . . . rather moved. Well, I'd better go and change

He exits to the staircase. A crash, off.

Birkett   The step, Mr Headingley, sir, the step!

Buckle *enters right, wearing a dinner jacket. He is a ponderous man of great loyalty, character, independence, and presence, who thinks everything out for himself and is a very impressive father to his children.*

Birkett   Mr Buckle.

Buckle   Is there, Mr Birkett, somewhere in this vicinity, a gentleman who goes by name of Christopher Headingley?

Birkett   In his old rooms, Mr Buckle, sir. G2. Arrived scarcely one moment past.

Buckle   In his old rooms. We're all in our old rooms, are we, Mr Birkett?

Birkett   You are, Mr Buckle, sir.

Buckle   In his old rooms. What a curiously pleasant sound those words have! I rather think I should like them carved on my grave.

Headingley *opens the window of a ground-floor room and leans out.*

Headingley   David Buckle!

Buckle   Christopher Headingley!

Headingley *vanishes.*

Birkett   And what a day we have for it, Mr Buckle!

Buckle   What a day indeed, Mr Birkett.

Birkett *exits left.* **Headingley** *enters from the staircase door with a towel round his shoulders.*

Headingley   Good heavens!

Buckle   My word!

Headingley   Well, well, well!

Buckle   Great Scott!

Headingley   Good God!

Buckle   How very odd to see you again like this, Christopher!

Headingley   How very odd to see *you.*

Buckle   Goodness me.

Headingley   Well, how are you, and so on?

Buckle   Well, all right, Christopher. Not too bad. In quite good working order. And you?

Headingley   Fine. Fine, fine, fine.

Buckle   Good, good, good.

Headingley   Yes, fine. And you're – sawing people up?

Buckle   Whhht! Out with their waterworks!

Headingley   My word.

Buckle   And you're – Parliamentary Under-Secretary, is that what they call it – at the Department of – isn't it in fact Education?

Headingley   Whhht! Off with their heads!

Buckle   Goodness me.

Headingley   Tell the Vice-Chancellor where he gets off.

Buckle   Well, well, well. It's funny, you know. You haven't changed at all.

Headingley   Nor have you! Isn't it odd?

Buckle   I ran into Tubby Rogers in First Court. He hasn't changed, either. It's curious. You don't expect people to have changed. But when you meet them and they haven't, you're somehow surprised.

Headingley   Isn't it odd?

Buckle   I mean, we all *have* changed.

Headingley   There's rather more of us.

Buckle   More of us?

Headingley   In some ways. (*He pats his stomach.*)

Buckle   Yes, though of course in other ways rather less of us.

Headingley   Yes. Poor old Ted.

Buckle   Poor old Jimmy.

Headingley   Jimmy?

Buckle   Jimmy McBride.

Headingley No!

Buckle Heart.

Headingley I didn't know that.

Buckle And drink, of course.

Headingley Then there's poor old Arthur.

Buckle Yes, poor old Arthur.

Headingley Shock of my life.

Buckle Never have imagined.

Headingley Never have dreamt.

Buckle What was it, in the end?

Headingley Five years.

Buckle Such rotten luck.

Headingley But how funny being back here!

Buckle The things you remember and the things you don't.

Headingley Like the way the bird droppings catch old Henry's nose.

Buckle Green man with a white nose.

Headingley They stand on his head.

Buckle Pigeons, mostly.

Headingley Always arse-about-face, for some reason.

Buckle Then, suddenly . . .

Headingley Woomph.

Buckle Bombs away.

Headingley Used to watch them for hours, sometimes. I'd think, I'll just watch one load go, then I'll get down to work. I'd wait . . . wait . . . wait . . . Then at the crucial moment I'd blink.

Buckle   But there was time for those things then.

Headingley   You know, I can't help wondering if one didn't learn quite a lot from that kind of thing.

Buckle   One had time to really look closely at something.

Headingley   Even if it was only a pigeon crapping. Funny. I haven't thought about those pigeon-droppings for twenty years.

Buckle   But as soon as you saw them . . .

Headingley   I just kind of went on from where I'd left off.

Snell *enters left. He is an anxious man with a beard, an open-necked shirt, bicycle clips on his trousers, a rucksack on his back and a camera round his neck.*

Snell   Excuse me.

Buckle   Can we help you?

Snell   What do you do, exactly?

Headingley   What, here?

Buckle   In College?

Snell   I'm sorry to trouble you.

Headingley   That's all right. What do we do, David?

Buckle   Watch the pigeons?

Headingley   That kind of thing. Reflect on life.

Buckle   Slosh about the river after lunch.

Headingley   I seem to remember going to some things called lectures.

Buckle   Come on, now, Chris, no boasting.

Headingley (*to* **Snell**)   And don't forget to look in the Chapel.

Buckle   There's a painting in there by some fearfully famous painter.

Headingley   Beethoven or somebody.

They resume their conversation with each other.

Headingley (*to* **Buckle**)   I nearly didn't come, you know. Terrible idea usually, reunions.

Snell *exits through an archway, up left, uncertainly.*

Buckle   I had the odd qualm.

Headingley   But now I've actually got here, and seen the old place again . . .

Buckle   Seen you, and Tubby Rogers . . .

Headingley   And old Birkett. And King Henry . . .

Buckle   And Jock Stewart, and . . . (*He glances off left. His tone changes.*) And Alan Quine.

Headingley   Oh, no!

Quine *and* **Birkett** *enter left.* **Quine**, *also carrying a weekend bag, is a man of conservative appearance, sardonic manner and anarchic character, whose chief pleasure in life is making others feel ill at ease.*

Birkett   This way, Mr Quine, sir, if you please.

Buckle   Hello, Alan! Remember me?

Quine   Yes.

Buckle   David Buckle.

Quine   Yes.

Headingley   Hello, Alan.

Quine   Minister.

Headingley   Oh balls. None of that nonsense here.

Buckle   How are you these days, Alan?

Quine   Fine. (*He looks around.*)

Birkett   Doesn't change much, does it, Mr Quine, sir?

Quine   It doesn't change at all, Mr Birkett.

Birkett   Mr Headingley said the same thing.

Buckle   I think I made the same remark.

Quine   It still looks . . . as much like Wormwood Scrubs as ever.

Headingley   Well done, Alan.

Birkett   Always a joke on his lips, always a humorous remark. I said to the Master, as soon as I saw Mr Quine's name on the list, I said, 'Oh, he'll be making a crack or two about us before the weekend's out!' You're not forgotten, you see, Mr Quine.

Quine   Dead but not forgotten.

Buckle   You married, Alan?

Quine   Occasionally.

Headingley   Children?

Quine   Every other Sunday.

Birkett   Oh, Mr Quine does pull our legs, doesn't he, Mr Headingley? Now, Mr Quine, I've put you in G4. Your old rooms, Mr Quine, sir.

Quine   My old rooms? Haven't they made a start on slum clearance here yet?

Birkett   Anyway, we've a beautiful day for it. Not even you can deny that, Mr Quine.

Quine   The trouble about having a beautiful day for something, Mr Birkett, is that it would be just as beautiful for something else.

Birkett   Where should we be without you to put us all in our places, Mr Quine?

Quine *goes into the stairs.*

Birkett   We might all start enjoying ourselves.

He exits left.

Buckle   I'd forgotten Quine, I must admit.

Headingley   I hadn't. He's in my Department. He's one of my civil servants.

Buckle   Oh dear. In the Department of Education? In charge of educating people?

Headingley   I don't know what he does. Puts the splinters in schoolroom benches, probably.

Buckle   Oh, I dare say he's grown up a bit since we knew him.

Headingley   He was very immature.

Buckle   Callow.

Headingley   Out to shock.

Buckle   I always thought he might have been all right if one could have got him on his own.

Headingley   He was in a rather nasty set.

Buckle   What was that appalling little man called?

Headingley   That ghastly camp little man?

Sainsbury *enters right, wearing a dinner jacket and a clerical collar.*

Sainsbury   Look at you both! With the mulberry tree in the background! What a picture!

Buckle   Dicky Sainsbury.

Headingley   We were just talking about you.

Sainsbury   How flattering. And you're both looking radiant. Isn't it all wonderful, being back? All those embarrassingly familiar faces, like the old shoes at the bottom of the wardrobe. Isn't it just absolutely frightful? So what's the score?

Buckle   I think it's about 180 for five.

Sainsbury   Children! How many children?!

Headingley   Oh.

Sainsbury   You want to tell me about your children, don't you?

Buckle   Two. Two boys.

Headingley   Three boys.

Sainsbury   Oh, well done! Five more members of the Boat Club on their way!

Snell *enters up left.*

Snell   No, sorry, I mean, where do you go?

Buckle   Where do you . . . ?

Sainsbury   I'll show you. This way. It's next to the Porter's Lodge. (*To* **Headingley** *and* **Buckle**, *indicating his collar.*) My pastoral role!

Sainsbury *and* **Snell** *exit left.*

Buckle   Dicky Sainsbury.

Headingley   Dicky Sainsbury.

Buckle   It all comes back to one, doesn't it?

Headingley   With a rush.

Buckle   I suppose he might have changed.

Headingley   It hardly looks like it.

Buckle   You mean the pretend dog collar?

Headingley   We're supposed to be shocked, are we?

Buckle   I expect when he sees we're not he'll go and take it off.

Headingley   Yes, probably. Take everything off.

Buckle   You're thinking of that show that he and Quine got up.

Headingley   The time the Queen Mother came.

Buckle And he came prancing on in nothing but false eyelashes and a coat of gold paint.

Headingley And we all found ourselves on page one of the Sunday papers.

Buckle He's coming back.

Sainsbury *enters left.* **Headingley** *and* **Buckle** *start to go off right.*

Sainsbury Someone told me you were the Prime Minister.

Headingley Not quite, I'm afraid.

Sainsbury No? Oh, well, it must have been someone else.

Headingley *and* **Buckle** *exit right.* **Quine** *enters from the staircase with a towel.*

Sainsbury Alan!

Quine God Almighty!

Sainsbury No, but what a flattering mistake.

Quine What's that thing round your neck?

Sainsbury Oh, I thought no one was ever going to ask! You don't think it makes me look old?

Quine It makes you look like a clergyman.

Sainsbury Only I keep catching sight of myself in shop windows and thinking I just look like someone dressed up as a clergyman.

Quine You are someone dressed up as a clergyman.

Sainsbury Yes, but underneath I am in fact a clergyman!

Quine No, you're not.

Sainsbury Yes, I am! It's in my passport!

Quine You read Geography.

Sainsbury   I'm a late vocation! Honestly! I solemnise weddings!

Quine   You couldn't solemnise a boiled egg.

Sainsbury   I baptise babies! I church women!

Quine   I should never have come. I knew it would be a disaster.

Sainsbury   Alan, why didn't you keep in touch? Why didn't you write? I wrote to you. I wrote and wrote. Told you how I was going mad at home. How I was going to emigrate to Canada and become a lumberjack. But not a word back from you.

Quine   There wasn't anything to say.

Sainsbury   Nothing's happened to you? In quarter of a century? Nothing at all?

Quine   Well . . .

Sainsbury   Ah! There *was* something!

Quine   One day . . .

Sainsbury   Yes?

Quine   About five years ago . . .

Sainsbury   Go on.

Quine   I was in Manchester . . .

Sainsbury   Manchester, yes, Manchester. I know Manchester.

Quine   And somewhere – in someone's office, maybe – or in a taxi . . .

Sainsbury   Something happened.

Quine   I left my raincoat behind.

Sainsbury   You left your raincoat behind?

Quine   I think so.

Sainsbury   Well, thank you for sharing that with me. You feel easier in yourself, too, don't you, now you've told someone about it.

Snell *enters right, uncertainly.*

Sainsbury (*to* **Snell**)   No? Something else I can do for you? Marry you? Bury you?

Snell   I don't know where I'm supposed to be. I was in lodgings before, you see.

Sainsbury   So what are you in now?

Snell (*baffled*)   What am I in now? I'm in ethical pharmaceuticals.

Sainsbury   I think I should go back to the lodgings.

Snell   Just as well I brought my bicycle.

Headingley *and* **Buckle** *enter right.*

Sainsbury (*to* **Headingley** *and* **Buckle**)   Perfect day for it! Or have we already squeezed about as much as we can out of the weather?

Quine *and* **Sainsbury** *exit right.*

Headingley   Oh dear. Oh dear, oh dear, oh dear.

Buckle   We'll just have to try and look on the bright side. Remember Tubby Rogers is here. And Mike Sims and Mark Samuels . . .

Tate *enters left, in his dinner jacket. He is a comfortable, cosy man, with a womanly manner and a little moustache.*

Headingley   . . . and Norman Tate!

Tate   Hello, Chris. Hello, David. Just popping round to say hello to everyone.

Buckle   Well, well, well! Auntie Norman!

Tate   I say, you haven't changed at all, you two. Five children, me! Isn't it awful? Five girls! Would you believe it? Oh, but I'm terribly pleased, really. Having children does teach you such a jolly awful lot. Well, how are you both? Are you both lovely and well? No little sniffles or snuffles?

Headingley   Not too bad, thank you, Norman.

Buckle   Plodding along.

Tate   That's the ticket.

Headingley   And you?

Tate   Oh, I'm lovely. A rather naughty old knee that gets the sulks every now and then. But we just have to be brave soldiers about that kind of thing, don't we, and think about something else. Anyway, we can't complain about the weather today, can we?

Buckle   No, we've certainly picked the right day for it.

Tate   Well, I don't need to ask what you two are getting up to these days, because you're both frightfully famous. But I bet you don't know what I do.

Headingley   What do you do, Norman?

Tate   I'm a writer!

Headingley   I didn't know you had literary leanings.

Tate   No, I just suddenly blossomed out. Children's novels, light verse, celebrity confessions for the Sunday papers . . .

Headingley   How about doing the confessions of a famous surgeon?

Buckle   Or a future Prime Minister?

Tate   Well, I'd love to, of course. I've done some quite famous people already. One or two very well-known naughty ladies. Oh, I love it! It really takes you out of yourself.

Buckle   I can see we're going to have to watch our step tonight, Chris.

Headingley   Yes, or we'll be right back in the Sunday papers.

Tate   No, but seriously, if you ever do want a professional hand with anything . . . (*He gives them each a card.*) Well, put it behind the clock just in case. I must be slipping along. I want to pop my head in on Roddy Moore.

Buckle   Roddy Moore?

Headingley   Roddy Moore's coming?

Tate   I looked at the list. He's in his old rooms!

Buckle   Oh, well, if old Roddy's coming, that's different.

Headingley   Old Roddy'll make the party go.

Tate   I didn't think he'd come!

Buckle   I was sure he wouldn't!

Headingley   Not like Roddy, to come to a thing like this.

Buckle   But how like Roddy, to do something that's not like him!

Headingley   Let's all go up and give him a surprise.

Tate   G staircase! Upstairs! G3!

Buckle   I think the last time I heard of him he was working with a construction gang in Anatolia.

Headingley   I heard he was selling Rolex watches off a barrow on Forty-Second Street.

Sainsbury and **Quine** *enter right.*

Sainsbury   Would you believe it? The lovely Auntie Norman!

Headingley and **Buckle** *exit to the staircase.*

Tate   Hello, Dicky! Hello, Alan!

Sainsbury   And looking younger than ever.

Tate   Oh, I don't know about that!

Sainsbury   No, no, no – you don't look a day over fifty.

Tate   Well, goodness me, I'm forty-seven!

Sainsbury   Yes, but you see, Norman, when you were twenty it was sixty you didn't look a day over.

Tate (*puzzled*)   Dicky . . .

Sainsbury   What's that thing round my neck? That thing round my neck is a joke clergyman's kit. I bought it in Woolworths this afternoon. It cost one pound ninety-nine and it's washable.

Tate   Well, I can see you two haven't changed.

Sainsbury   Don't go on, Norman. Don't get started. Leave us in peace. Just say something profound before you go. Something short, and deep, and strange, and curiously consoling. The rich distillate of half a lifetime. Record your message now.

Tate   I was just going to say that Roddy Moore's coming.

Sainsbury (*delighted*)   Roddy Moore! Did you hear that, Alan? Well done, Norman! That's very short and deep and strange. (*To* **Quine**.) Roddy Moore! That alters the picture a bit!

Quine (*brightening*)   Roddy wouldn't come to a thing like this, would he? It would mean speaking to people. He can't have started *saying* things!

Tate   I looked at the list!

Sainsbury   It's rather improbable. He was last seen meditating in Nepal.

Quine   I thought he was doing a milk round in Kentish Town?

Tate   He's down on the list! He's in his old rooms!

Quine   Come on, then. Let's go up and mock him.

Buckle *enters from the staircase.*

Tate   How's Roddy, then? Silent as ever?

Buckle   Totally. Hasn't even arrived yet.

Tate   Late as ever! He hasn't changed, then!

Buckle   Well, I'm going to trot along to the Fellows' Garden and have some sherry.

Sainsbury   David, do you realise you still haven't asked me how many children I've got?

Buckle   I'm terribly sorry! I thought . . . I simply assumed . . . So you're married, then, are you, Dicky?

Quine *laughs, and exits to the staircase.*

Sainsbury   No, David, but it was sweet of you to ask.

Buckle   I'll see you later.

He exits right.

Tate   I always thought it was an awful pity that you and Alan didn't get on better with people like David and Chris. I wish I could get you together. I'd feel I'd really done a bit of good in the world.

Taylor *enters left, on a bicycle. He is in his twenties, and is informally dressed.*

Sainsbury   What's this? A real live undergraduate.

Tate   I wonder what he's doing here?

Sainsbury   Did we look like that once? Did we look that *young*?

Taylor *exits to the staircase.*

Tate   I suppose he's going to see his tutor. (*He looks at the list of names at the foot of the staircase.*) G1. Dr W. R. Taylor. He's new since our day.

Sainsbury   They shouldn't have left any real ones about. It ruins the illusion.

Birkett *enters left, carrying a tray of sherry.*

Birkett   Sweet or dry, Mr Sainsbury, sir? Sweet or dry, Mr Tate, sir?

Sainsbury   You were never young, were you, Mr Birkett?

Birkett   Certainly not, Mr Sainsbury, sir. I was far too busy.

Sainsbury   You were a silver-haired old retainer already when we were up.

Tate   And that was twenty-five years ago, so you must have been . . .

Sainsbury (*appalled realisation*)   Not much older than we are now.

Tate   Good heavens!

Birkett   This way, then, Mr Sainsbury, sir, Mr Tate, sir. You'll find them all foregathering in the Fellows' Garden.

Sainsbury *and* **Tate** *exit right.* **Taylor** *enters from the staircase.*

Birkett   Sweet or dry, Dr Taylor, sir?

Taylor (*helps himself to sherry*)   What's this lot, then, Sydney? Car salesmen's convention?

Birkett   This is the Gathering of Old Members, Dr Taylor, sir. We hold them every Long Vacation.

Taylor   Oh, these are our kids, are they?

Birkett   They came up twenty-five years ago.

Taylor   Back in for servicing?

Birkett   Every twenty-five years, Dr Taylor, sir.

Taylor   Check the sherry levels. Top up the port.

Birkett   A little discreet flattery is usually appreciated.

Taylor   And banker's order forms to follow.

Birkett   The new building has to be paid for somehow.

Taylor   They're not bad, are they, Sydney? They have what some of us in the English Department would call authenticity.

Birkett   I think one might say, Dr Taylor, sir, that they have body. A matter of bottle-age.

Taylor   Were they convincing as undergraduates?

Birkett   Not particularly.

Taylor   Look after them, then, Sydney. Make sure they don't get their sediment shaken up.

He turns to exit, then remembers something.

But the industrial action, Sydney, the industrial action! The Joint Action Committee banned overtime working!

Birkett   As of midnight, Dr Taylor, sir.

Taylor   As of midnight. On the stroke of twelve the spell will be broken, and nothing but the odd crystal slipper will remain.

Birkett   And you won't forget you're down to say grace?

Taylor *waves his assent and exits to the staircase.* **Lady Driver** *enters right, scooting herself along on an ancient upright bicycle with a disintegrating basket that contains books and papers, and her practical and capacious shoulder-bag. She is a busy, organising woman in her forties, wearing spectacles and sensible clothes.*

Lady Driver   Mr Birkett . . .

Birkett   Your ladyship.

Lady Driver   Is everything under control?

Birkett   Perfectly, your ladyship.

Lady Driver   The sherry's holding out?

Birkett   Most assuredly.

Lady Driver   You have chilled the hock, and warmed the claret, and opened the Sauternes? And decanted the port, and fetched up the brandy? And put the whisky in the Old Library for afterwards? And broached the beer for when the whisky runs out?

Birkett   Yes, yes, yes, yes, yes, and yes again.

Lady Driver   And your overtime ban begins at midnight. You will make sure that they've drunk their way through the complete list first? They've waited twenty-five years for this. They'll be seventy before they get their next go. I don't want them to miss anything just because Harry's away.

Birkett   Even if the Master were here, I think there's little more he could offer them without a considerable risk of alcoholic poisoning.

Lady Driver   And you'll lock up before you go?

Birkett   Every lockable lock, your ladyship. Every boltable bolt.

Lady Driver   Keep trouble in.

Birkett   In it will be absolutely kept.

Lady Driver   And the public out.

Birkett   Out they will absolutely remain.

Snell *enters left, uncertainly.*

Lady Driver   If people come wandering in and see nothing but a lot of drunken hooligans capering about in dinner jackets they may not realise that this is . . .

Snell   Excuse me. I don't know what I'm supposed to be doing.

Lady Driver   . . . one of the more progressive colleges.

Birkett   I do apologise, your ladyship. (*To* **Snell**.) I'm afraid the College is closed to visitors this evening, sir.

Snell   I can't find my lodgings. There's a shopping centre there.

Birkett   This way, if you please, sir. Have you tried the youth hostel?

Birkett *and* **Snell** *exit left.*

Lady Driver *makes to exit to the staircase. She props her bicycle, removes her spectacles, takes her bag out of the bicycle basket, and puts her* *spectacles into it.* **Headingley** *enters from the staircase, now changed into his dinner jacket.*

Headingley Rosemary!

Lady Driver *(replacing her spectacles)* Oh – hello, Christopher.

Headingley *(shaking hands)* Well, well, well! This is a surprise!

Lady Driver Yes! What a surprise!

Headingley I keep meeting Harry, of course, at committees and conferences. But we haven't met for – what . . . ?

Lady Driver Twenty-two years.

Headingley No!

Lady Driver When Harry and I got married.

Headingley You've become younger, obviously.

Lady Driver And you've become the Minister in charge of us all.

Headingley Isn't it ridiculous? When you consider I got a third?

Lady Driver Anyway, here you are, returning in triumph.

Headingley But how sweet of you to pop round and say hello!

Lady Driver Oh, well . . .

Headingley Oh, you weren't.

Lady Driver I really just wanted to say one thing. I know Harry would have liked to ask you round to the Lodge for a quiet drink at some point.

Headingley How nice. What time?

Lady Driver But sadly he's away this weekend.

Headingley Oh, Harry's away, is he?

Lady Driver He's in Montreal.

Headingley   So no quiet drink?

Lady Driver   I thought I ought to rush round and explain.

Headingley   How very kind.

Lady Driver (*taking hold of her bicycle*)   Well, I must dash off. With Harry away I've been left to sprint round and organise everything.

Headingley   I remember that bicycle, don't I?

He runs his hand familiarly over the basket and its contents.

Lady Driver   Oh, this old thing.

Headingley   Many's the time I saw you wheeling it into College, on your way to have tea with some lucky man.

Lady Driver   Yes. I've had quite a lot of use out of it.

Headingley   You'd carefully lock it up. Take the pump off it. Gather up a great armful of notes and files from the basket. Then you'd take your glasses off and put them in your bag.

Lady Driver   You should have read History. You might have got a first.

Headingley   I used to watch you out of my window.

Lady Driver   I suppose I was rather noticeable. There were no women in College in those days.

Headingley   Look, Rosemary . . . (*His hands come to rest with his fingers inside the bicycle basket.*) . . . why don't we have a drink and a bit of a chat later on, anyway? I can see old Harry any time. Come round after dinner. I'm in my old rooms.

Lady Driver   Christopher, I've . . . changed a lot since you knew me.

Headingley (*hastily snatches his hands away from the basket*)   Oh, good heavens, Rosemary, I didn't mean *that*!

Lady Driver   No, no, no, no, no, no! *I* didn't mean *that*!

Headingley   I mean, *I've* changed!

Lady Driver   Yes, yes, yes, yes, yes! I didn't mean you meant *that*.

Headingley   I meant, to have a chat about old times.

Lady Driver   Yes, yes, yes, yes, yes! I mean, it might not be quite the thing for the Master's wife to be flittering about people's rooms in the middle of the night.

Headingley   Of course not.

Lady Driver   Given the circumstances.

Headingley   You mean, because of Roddy?

Lady Driver   Because of Roddy? What do you mean, because of Roddy?

Headingley   Well, you had this great thing with Roddy . . .

Lady Driver   I can't see what it's got to do with Roddy.

Headingley   And then suddenly you married Harry . . .

Lady Driver   But why are you talking about *Roddy*?

Headingley   Oh dear, have I put my foot in it again?

Lady Driver   I haven't seen Roddy for twenty years. I don't suppose I shall ever see him again.

Headingley   Rosemary, I'm terribly sorry.

Lady Driver   Why should I care what Roddy thinks?

Headingley   I just thought you might find it slightly . . .

Lady Driver   Well, I don't.

Headingley   Oh dear. I seem to have said all the wrong things.

Lady Driver   You always did. I can't think how you ever became a politician.

Headingley   No. Anyway, let me put it like this. *If* you happen to be passing this way after dinner . . .

Lady Driver   I shan't be.

Headingley   And *if* by any chance you happen to feel like a chat . . .

Lady Driver   I shall be in bed and fast asleep.

Headingley   Well, you know where I am.

Lady Driver   I know where you are.

Headingley   Let's leave it like that, then.

Lady Driver   Let's leave it like that.

Headingley   Well, nice to have seen you again, Rosemary. I always admired you from a distance, you know.

Lady Driver   I remember. Well, I must dash along and chase things up.

Headingley   Yes, and I must rush along and drink some sherry.

He exits right, in some slight confusion.

Lady Driver *exits left – almost. Then, seeing that* **Headingley** *is safely out of the way, she returns to the door of the staircase, props her bicycle, takes off her spectacles and puts them in her bag.*

Quine *enters from the staircase, wearing his dinner jacket.*

Quine   Rosemary!

Lady Driver (*putting on her spectacles*)   Oh, hello, Alan! How nice to see you again!

Quine   Rosemary Gilbert!

Lady Driver   Well, Rosemary Driver now, of course.

Quine   Oh yes. You married that don with the loud laugh who used to come to Dicky's parties.

Lady Driver   Harry Driver.

Quine   Sir Harry Driver.

Lady Driver   As he now is.

Quine   So you're – the Lady Driver?

Lady Driver   I didn't know he was going to get knighted when I married him.

Quine   And now he's Master of the College. Which makes you, what? – the College Mistress?

Lady Driver   I see you haven't changed much, Alan.

Quine   Well, come in, Rosemary, come in.

Lady Driver   Oh . . . Well . . .

Quine   It was me you were calling on, was it?

Lady Driver   Yes . . . yes . . .

Quine   It wasn't.

Lady Driver   I was just going to look in for a moment.

Quine   You weren't on your way up to see Roddy?

Lady Driver   Why should I want to see Roddy?

Quine   *I* don't know. Tell him it was all a terrible mistake and it was him you should have married after all.

Lady Driver   You can't still be bitter.

Quine   I'm not bitter. Not at all. Sentimental, if anything. I remember the last time I saw you. You were wearing a long white dress.

Lady Driver   Oh, that white taffeta ballgown . . .

Quine   It was a warm summer's night, and the moon was shining. I looked out of my bedroom window at the back here, and there you were. Dangling on the wall with your dress caught on the spikes.

Lady Driver   Oh, then . . .

Quine   You were climbing in to see Roddy.

Lady Driver   It finished the dress off. I suppose it served me right. I'd been to a ball somewhere with some dreadful creepy man, and run out on them halfway through.

Quine   Yes. Me.

Lady Driver   No!

Quine   Yes.

Lady Driver   Oh dear.

Quine   Yes.

Lady Driver   I suppose I behaved badly to everyone that year.

Quine   Yes.

Lady Driver   It was my last year. I wanted to somehow . . . get hold of it all before it disappeared.

Quine   You got hold of half this College.

Lady Driver   There were ten men to every woman at the University in those days. You have to remember that.

Quine   You fought gallantly against hopeless odds.

Lady Driver   That's what it felt like sometimes. You don't realise.

Quine   I'd look out of my window and see you pushing your bike into the court . . .

Lady Driver   I could feel everyone peering down at me. It was like walking onto a stage.

Quine   You'd carefully lock up the bike. Then you'd take your glasses off. The whole College must have been nothing but a myopic blur. A haze of honey-brown stone . . . So, you ditched Roddy, and married Harry Driver, and stayed here, and took over the whole College.

Lady Driver   So much for my life. How about yours?

Quine   Come and have a drink after dinner, and I'll tell you.

Lady Driver   Oh, I can't, I'm afraid.

Quine   Busy?

Lady Driver   Well, Harry's away . . .

Quine   We'll manage without Harry.

Lady Driver   Alan, I'm an entirely different sort of person now.

Quine   Oh.

Lady Driver   I sit on committees. I'm on the Bench.

Quine   Not in the middle of the night, surely?

Lady Driver   I must go.

Quine   Don't you want to see if Roddy's arrived yet?

Lady Driver *exits left.*

Quine   I'll keep a light in the window for you!

He exits right. **Lady Driver** *enters left. She props her bicycle by the door and removes her spectacles.* **Birkett** *and* **Snell** *enter left.*

Birkett   Well, well, well! Fancy our forgetting *you*!

Snell   Oh, I don't suppose anyone remembers me.

Birkett   I never forget a name and I never forget a face. But we've left you off the list, you see. That's what's happened, Mr . . .

Snell   Snell. Kenneth Snell.

Lady Driver (*putting on her spectacles and taking up her bicycle*) Trouble, Mr Birkett?

Birkett   Your ladyship. Would you believe it, we've left Mr . . .

Snell   Snell.

Birkett   . . . Mr Snell off the list.

Snell   I'm sorry. I sent in the form.

Birkett (*consulting his clipboard*)   Let me see, where can we put you?

Snell   I never had rooms in College. I should have had them in my third year, but I got left off the list. I was out in lodgings all the time. I don't suppose anyone realised I was a member of the College. I expect that's the trouble.

Lady Driver   So, if you'll find a room for Mr . . .

Snell   Snell.

Birkett   Leave it to me, your ladyship.

Lady Driver   I'll hare along and tell the kitchens.

She exits left on her bicycle.

Birkett   I have it, sir, I have it. We'll put you in G3. Mr Moore's old rooms.

Snell   Roddy Moore's old rooms? Isn't he coming, then?

Birkett   We've just had a message. Apparently his analyst has advised against it. This way, Mr Snell, sir. Up the stairs, and on your left. You've just time to dress for dinner.

Snell   Thank you, Mr Birkett. It's very kind of you to fit me in.

Birkett *exits left.* **Snell** *watches him go. His manner changes. He suddenly snatches off one shoe and does a high martial arts kick in* **Birkett***'s direction, with an accompanying noise.* **Birkett** *enters left.*

Birkett   You called, Mr Snell, sir?

Snell (*his former self again*)   Called? I didn't call.

Birkett   I beg your pardon, Mr Snell, sir. And I shall be ringing the bell for Hall in two minutes.

Snell   Thank you, Mr Birkett.

Birkett *exits right.*

Snell   Speaking to myself – that's the accusation now, is it? They've tried that one on me before, and it doesn't scare *me*.

He exits to the staircase, shoe in hand. **Lady Driver** *enters left, and props her bicycle by the door. She looks around very carefully and removes her spectacles. An upstairs window is flung open and* **Lady Driver** *looks up.* **Snell** *is briefly visible. She waves, but already he is gone. She takes the bag out of the basket and makes to go in.*

Taylor *enters from the staircase, wearing his dinner jacket and gown.*

Taylor   Rosemary!

Lady Driver (*despairing*)   What now . . . ? (*She replaces her spectacles.*) Oh, it's you.

Taylor   I can't ask you in. I'm due in Hall to say grace.

Lady Driver   Never mind. Another time.

Taylor   I know what you're after, Rosemary.

Lady Driver   Do you? I'm beginning to wonder.

Taylor   And the answer's no.

Lady Driver   No?

Taylor   No.

Lady Driver   Oh.

Taylor   Well, you've come to seduce me, haven't you?

Lady Driver   I'm beginning to have the feeling that life has caught up with me.

Taylor   No, come on. Harry sent you.

Lady Driver   Harry sent me? To seduce you?

Taylor   Away from the Joint Action Committee. To stop the industrial action.

Lady Driver   Oh, the industrial action.

Taylor   Well, it won't work, Rosemary. The time has come for the academic and domestic staff to show solidarity.

Lady Driver   Look, Harry's not even here.

Taylor   Harry's not here?

Lady Driver   He's in Montreal.

Taylor (*thinking*)   Well, all right. Come round for a drink after Hall. There'll be no one to disturb us.

A bell begins to toll, off.

And you can have a go.

Lady Driver   Hall, William.

Taylor   You can do your worst.

Lady Driver   *Benedictus benedicat.*

Taylor   What?

Lady Driver   Grace, William.

Taylor   Oh, yes.

He begins to go off left. She waits for him to go.

(*Calls.*) But I warn you, Rosemary – I'll have you on the floor!

Exit **Taylor** *left.* **Lady Driver** *looks round to see if anyone has heard this last remark. She props her bicycle by the staircase once again, then stops at the sound of a burble of approaching festive voices. She flees to the staircase as* **Headingley** *and the others, together with as many extra* **Old Members** *as there are understudies to play them, begin to surge across the Court, right to left, all in genial mood.*

Headingley   The bell for Hall! Isn't that the sweetest sound you ever heard?

Old Member   Hall for all, and all for Hall!

Headingley   Lead on, Macduff! Where's Tubby? Come on, Tubby! Grub up!

Old Members   Good heavens, it's Jock and Jimmy . . . ! Well well well well well . . . !

The front wall of the college comes in as the burble of social conversation continues and merges into a confused roar.

Goodness me, Auntie Norman . . . ! My word! Good gracious! Rooky! Ricky . . . ! Mickey! Nicky . . . ! Bobby! Robby! Nobby . . . ! Heavens above! By all that's wonderful! Garry!

Harry! Larry . . . ! My my! Good grief! Good Lord! Tim!
Tom! Tam . . . ! Fred! Ned! Ted . . . ! Matt, Pat, Nat . . . ! Ken,
Ben, Den . . . ! Mark Samuels! – Bob Prentice! – I mean, Bob
Prentice . . . (*Etc., ad lib.*)

Snell, *hurrying after the others, and still changing into his dinner jacket,
comes through the open gate in the front wall to struggle with his tie in
private. The conversation continues from inside the Hall.* **Birkett**
*emerges from the gate with a large bunch of keys, locks it, and goes back
in through the little wicket door set in the gate.*

The sound of many men sitting down to dinner.

Snell *discovers that he has been excluded once again. He hammers on the
gate.* **Birkett** *unlocks the wicket and* **Snell** *hurries inside.* **Birkett**
comes out to check there's no one else outside.

The sound of a gavel. The roar of conversation dies away. **Birkett**
removes his hat.

Taylor (*off, indistinctly*)   *Benedictus benedicat, per Christum dominum
nostrum.* Amen.

Omnes   Amen.

The roar of conversation resumes. **Birkett** *takes out a banana and eats
it. Gathering darkness. The indistinct sounds of an introduction to a
speech, followed by the speech itself, given by* **Headingley**. **Birkett**
*laughs at the inaudible jokes, exactly like the audience inside, perhaps
silently gestures applause, even though we can't hear the words. He shakes
his head at what a card* **Headingley** *is, brushes his fingers, and
unlocks the wicket to let himself in.*

*The sounds of the dinner become louder and mixed with music – until the
front wall goes out to reveal . . .*

Scene Two

Snell's *room. Night.*

Two doors: one, in the rear wall, leads to the landing and stairs down, the other, in a side wall, leads to the bedroom. A window embrasure with a window seat and curtains.

Headingley, **Buckle**, *and* **Tate** *burst in from the stairs, in a haze of cigar smoke.*

Headingley   Roddy!

Buckle   Where are you, Roddy?

Tate   We *are* in the right room?

Buckle (*checks the number on the door*)   G3.

Headingley   Looked everywhere in Hall. Not a sign of him.

Tate   His stuff's all here.

Buckle   He must be here somewhere.

Tate   A rucksack! Honestly!

Headingley   Trust Roddy!

Tate   Bicycle clips!

Headingley   Rod the sod. Where *is* he?

Buckle   Hiding in the bedroom . . .

He opens the bedroom door to look, but at that moment the staircase door opens.

Tate   Here he is!

Buckle *closes the bedroom door.* **Sainsbury**, **Taylor** *and* **Quine** *enter from the stairs.*

Sainsbury   Oh, a party!

Headingley   Come in.

Sainsbury   We're looking for Roddy Moore.

Tate   *We're* looking for Roddy Moore!

Buckle   The Moore the merrier.

Headingley   Sit down. Make yourselves at home.

They settle round in chairs.

Tate   His things are here.

Buckle   He can't be far away.

Tate   Rucksack! Bicycle clips!

Sainsbury   Cycled here! From Nepal!

Quine   Alaska.

Buckle   I thought it was Turkey.

Sainsbury   I think it's Nepal.

Quine   I think it's Alaska.

Sainsbury   I think I'm pissed.

Tate   They did us awfully well, you know.

Buckle   They were very generous with the drink, I must say.

Tate   Awfully generous.

Buckle   Awfully good speech, Chris.

Headingley   Did it seem all right?

Tate   Oh, just the job.

Buckle   Awfully good story about our Irish friends.

Headingley   Wouldn't have given any offence, would it?

Tate   Oh, I don't think so.

Buckle   None of them here to be offended, are there?

Tate   And the weather held up.

Quine (*looking out of the window*)   Warm darkness and the scent of flowers.

Headingley   It's funny, you know. Alan and I sit up there in
London all week, talking about education in the abstract. And
sometimes it all seems very remote and theoretical. You wonder
whether it's really worth making such a song and dance over.
Then you come back here, for an occasion like this, and
suddenly you see what education's all about. Wouldn't you
agree, Alan?

Quine   What we need is free brandy in schools.

Tate   No, but seriously, though, I can't help envying chaps
like Bill here the academic life.

Sainsbury   They don't get as pissed as this every night. Do
you, Bill?

Tate   No, but we could all have stayed up – done a bit of
research – got ourselves lectureships. I can't help feeling we'd
all have been better people.

Taylor   My personal feeling is that we should burn the whole
place down and start again.

Sainsbury   You can still speak!

Buckle   It's a thought, certainly.

Sainsbury   We could take it as a starting point for discussion.

Headingley   The whole beauty of this place, you see, Bill, is
that it gives you the freedom to put forward ideas like that.

Taylor   My personal feeling is that we ought to be free of
that kind of freedom.

Buckle   That's a very fair point, Bill.

Headingley   Very fair point. But the thing is, we can sit here
and discuss whether we ought in fact to be sitting here or not
in a perfectly friendly way. This place is a melting-pot.
Different viewpoints – different races – different classes – they
come here, they sit down together over a jolly good dinner . . .

Buckle   Jolly good wine.

Headingley   Jolly good wine.

Sainsbury   Tell us a funny thing, David.

Snell   Oh. Sorry.

Headingley (*to* **Snell**)   Sit down, sit down.

Snell   Sorry. (*He sits.*)

Buckle   Well, I don't know, this may be obvious to everyone else, but it's just occurred to me as I sat here. When you look *back* on your life, it all seems to make some kind of sense.

Headingley   I'm with you so far, David.

Buckle   You can see how everything leads inevitably to everything else.

Headingley   Absolutely.

Buckle   But when you look *forwards* over your life, into the future, it doesn't seem inevitable at all.

Headingley   That's right, David. You've put your finger on something there.

Tate   It's certainly true of my life.

Headingley   He's on to something here, isn't he?

Tate   It certainly explains a lot about my life.

Snell   Yes, or take my life, for instance.

Buckle   And I'll tell you another funny thing.

Snell   My life has been dominated by parasitic worms.

Buckle   I'll tell you another funny thing.

Snell   And parasitic worms have led me inexorably into the small intestine.

Buckle   I'll tell you another funny thing.

Headingley   Tell us another funny thing, David.

Snell   Sorry.

Sainsbury   He's full of funny things tonight.

Tate   The last one was very funny.

Headingley   Go ahead, David.

Sainsbury   Prophesy unto us.

Buckle   Well, I don't know whether there's anything in this or not. But I was just thinking, as we all sat here – the thought simply occurred to me – that, well, *here we all are.*

Headingley   Go on.

Buckle   I think that's more or less it.

Headingley   Here we all are?

Buckle   It's just something that struck me. As I was explaining about the first funny thing. I just found myself thinking, here we all are. Here we all absolutely are.

Headingley   I think I follow.

Buckle   Here I am, being a medical man.

Headingley   Right.

Buckle   Here *you* are, being in the Government.

Headingley   I see that.

Snell   Here *I* am, in the small intestine.

Buckle   There was a time when we could have been anything.

Quine   Oh God, the things we were going to be!

Buckle   I could have gone into . . . some entirely different branch of medicine.

Snell   I could have gone into the oesophagus.

Headingley   I see what you mean. You mean, I could have taken the firm, and my brother could have gone into the House of Commons?

Buckle   But in fact you went into the House of Commons.

Headingley   Right.

Tate   And your brother runs the firm.

Headingley   Absolutely.

Sainsbury   In other words, it's become of us.

Headingley   Become of us?

Sainsbury   Didn't you ever wonder what would become of you?

Tate   Yes, but what *has* become of us?

Sainsbury   Heaven knows. But whatever it is, become of us it certainly has.

Buckle   You see what I'm driving at, though?

Headingley   Funny, when you come to think about it.

Tate   Very funny.

Quine   And very, very sad.

Snell   I find this whole discussion deeply interesting. Take me, for instance. I'm working on parasitic infestation of the small intestine. Now, I can trace my path into the small intestine. I can follow it step by step from when I was four years old, and I first observed regurgitation. A herring gull at Llandudno, in North Wales, as it happened, and curiously enough it was near Cardiff, in *South* Wales, that I first became involved with intestinal worms, which is the other strand of the story. Now, I can remember when I first got the job I thought, the possibilities are endless! The whole alimentary canal lies open to me! But then I became ever more closely bound up with worms, and the worms tied me to the small intestine. Was there a point where I could have broken free? Was there a moment when I could have said, 'No! I shall go back to my first love – the oesophagus'? Or, 'I shall move on, and broaden my horizons by striking out into the large intestine'? Don't misunderstand me – I'm very happy where I am. It's just that I do sometimes feel rather cramped. There are days when I look up and think, 'Am I going to spend the rest of my life between the duodenum and the ileum?'

Pause. They gaze at him.

Headingley   Are you drunk?

Snell   I don't drink.

Headingley   He's drunk.

Snell   I don't drink!

Headingley   Drunk as a fiddler.

Snell   An occasional glass of sherry, yes.

Headingley   There's something very odd about his manner.

Snell   I've no objection to other people drinking.

Headingley   Comes barging in here. Starts spouting some bollocks about his intestines.

Taylor   We're drunk, and he's sober. That's the trouble.

Headingley   Drunk? Who's drunk?

Buckle   You're drunk.

Headingley   I'm not drunk. Are you drunk?

Buckle   I'm not drunk.

Taylor   I'm not drunk, in point of fact.

Sainsbury   *I'm* drunk.

Headingley   We're not drunk at all. In fact I'm thirsty. That's what's wrong with me.

Buckle   There's a barrel of beer in the Buttery.

Tate   Oh, my word!

Buckle   It's tempting.

Headingley   It's certainly tempting. Bill, you're a drinking man, I can see. A barrel of beer in the Buttery, Bill. Is that what you would call a temptation?

Taylor   It's what I'd call alliteration.

Headingley   Who's going to come downstairs with me and commit alliteration?

Tate   What about Mr Birkett?

Buckle   Oh yes – Birkett'll be on the Buttery beat.

A knock at the door.

Headingley   Come in.

Birkett *enters. He is wearing informal clothes.*

Headingley   Birkett. Good God. What in heaven's name are you wearing?

Birkett   Is Dr Taylor here?

Buckle   This is Dr Taylor.

Birkett   Oh, Dr Taylor, sir, I'm off.

Taylor   Off?

Birkett   The overtime ban, Dr Taylor, sir.

Taylor   Oh, the overtime ban. Yes, we voted in favour of it.

Birkett   It has begun, Dr Taylor, sir.

Taylor   Has it? Well, full support, and so on, Sydney.

Birkett   Thank you, sir.

Taylor   Anything I can do?

Birkett   I believe you're the only Senior Member in College overnight, Dr Taylor.

Taylor   Leave it all to me, Sydney. I have control.

Birkett   The keys, Dr Taylor, sir. (*Hands them over.*) The College is safely sealed off from all contact with the outside world. I've also taken the precaution of locking the gate to the Master's Lodge. I wouldn't wish her ladyship to be troubled in any way. Good night, then, Dr Taylor. I'm leaving everything in your capable hands.

Taylor   I have control, Sydney, I have control.

Birkett Good night, gentlemen.

Taylor Good night, Sydney.

Tate Good night, Mr Birkett.

Birkett I'll be back at seven a.m.

Taylor Have a good weekend.

Birkett *exits.*

Headingley Have you ever seen anything like it? T-shirt!

Tate Jeans!

Buckle Trainers!

Headingley I mean, God knows, I have never belonged to the ranks of the Jeremiahs who go around shouting, 'What has happened to this country?' But what *has* happened to this country? Birkett – Birkett! – running about in the middle of the night in T-shirt and jeans!

Taylor Well, he's off, isn't he? He's taking industrial action. You don't want him to take industrial action in a bowler hat, do you?

Headingley Industrial action! Exactly! God knows, I have never been one of those people who resented the efforts of the ordinary working man to get a fair deal, but when someone like Birkett chucks down his tools at midnight and refuses to work a few hours overtime, I think we do have to stop and ask ourselves if what we're seeing in this country is not a complete moral collapse . . . Just a moment – if old Birkett's shoved off, we could break into the Buttery and steal that beer.

Buckle The Buttery bitter! Or do I mean the Bittery butter?

Taylor The Bittery . . . the Buttery . . . they're both locked up.

He holds up the keys to demonstrate. **Headingley** *takes them.*

Headingley Come on, men. Raiding party, fall in!

Buckle Burgle the Buttery!

Tate   Now, now! Naughty words!

Buckle   I mean, butter the Buggery!

Taylor   Now wait a moment . . .

Headingley, **Buckle** *and* **Tate** *exit to the stairs.*

Snell   What about us? Shall we do something? This is just the kind of thing I missed in lodgings. You don't think we should climb up somewhere? Put a chamberpot on something?

Quine   Yes, you go and put a chamberpot on something.

Sainsbury   Something very high and very beautiful.

Taylor *rises.*

Snell   Are you going to put a chamberpot on something?

Taylor   They just took the keys out of my hand!

He exits to the stairs.

Snell   Will he be all right on the stairs?

A crash, off.

Sainsbury   No.

Snell *exits to the stairs.*

Sainsbury   How do you feel it's shaping up so far?

Quine   Not too badly. Chris Headingley's speech was the high point.

Sainsbury   I thought he surpassed all reasonable hopes with that story about the Irishman and the contraceptive.

Quine   Our best bet for the later stages of the entertainment is this clown with the beard.

Sainsbury   You think he's got a good eye for the well-placed chamberpot?

Quine   No, I think he's got a good chance of getting himself thrown in the river.

Snell *enters.*

Sainsbury   We were just saying, they need someone like you around on this kind of occasion.

Snell   Oh, well, I thought I'd better go and pick him up.

Quine   Sit down. Have a drink.

Snell   I don't drink.

Quine   Just as well. There isn't anything to drink . . . Why don't we get the keys and knock off one or two of those bottles of whisky in the Old Library?

Sainsbury   Then we'll come back and watch developments at the party.

Snell   The party? What party?

Quine   This party. Roddy's party. Tell him, will you, if he turns up while we're gone?

Snell   This is just the kind of thing I missed in lodgings!

Sainsbury   Tell him to put out some toilet rolls.

Snell   Toilet rolls?

Quine   It's not going to be much of a party if they don't throw toilet rolls out of the window.

Snell   Toilet rolls. Right. Anything else?

Sainsbury   Can you swim?

Snell   Swim?

Quine   It may be the sort of party where there's swimming.

Snell   I haven't got my costume.

Sainsbury   You won't need a costume.

Snell   Swimming in the nude?

Quine   Certainly not.

Sainsbury   Swimming in a dinner jacket.

Snell   Ye gods!

Quine Come on, Dicky. The whisky.

Sainsbury *and* **Quine** *exit to the stairs.*

Snell (*excited*) Well . . . Bring on the dancing girls!

The bedroom door opens a crack. **Snell** *reacts and freezes.* **Lady Driver**'s *head cautiously emerges. She is not wearing her spectacles.*

Lady Driver (*softly*) Roddy . . . ?

Snell *gazes at her, transfixed.*

Lady Driver Have they all gone?

She comes out of the bedroom, and looks anywhere but at **Snell**. *Pause.*

Lady Driver So . . . Are you well? What are you up to? Are you married? How is everything . . . ?

Snell *recovers from his surprise and prepares to shape some answer, but she forestalls him.*

Lady Driver Sorry. Stupid questions. Stupid, stupid, stupid. But, well . . . how in fact *are* you?

Snell *braces himself to speak, but she at once interrupts him.*

Lady Driver Silence. Of course. I should have known.

Snell *opens his mouth again.*

Lady Driver No! If you don't want to say anything, don't! You haven't said anything for twenty-two years! You never said anything before! Why start now? This is why everyone was so impressed by you – because you just stood there and grinned and didn't *say* anything . . . Look, I did *write* to you to tell you I was getting married! I wrote you a long letter! Look, look . . .

She scrabbles in her bag.

 Poured my heart out, as a matter of fact . . .

She pulls out an unopened envelope.

About you, about me. About everything. And all right, I didn't send it – it was at the bottom of my bag – I was getting married – I had a million things to do – I found it afterwards –

by which time it was rather out of date – and of course that was wrong – that was unforgiveable – and I'm sorry, I'm sorry! I've said – I'm sorry . . . !

Snell *tries again.*

Lady Driver Anyway, the engagement *was* announced in *The Times*.

And again.

And don't worry – I haven't come to have some terrible nostalgic scene! I never think about the past. I'm far too busy with the present. I just came to see how you are and tell you how I am, and I'm fine . . . (*She weeps.*) I'm very happy . . . It's just that I've been sitting in there for an hour expecting every moment to have someone come crashing in . . . Feeling such a fool . . . I didn't *plan* to be hiding in the bedroom! It never occurred to me that you might bring some horde of people back here after dinner . . . You *must* have expected to see me! You must have worked out what you were going to say! Well, say it, say it!

And again.

Or have you just completely forgotten about me . . . ?

Snell *makes yet another attempt to explain. She looks at him.*

Lady Driver That beard is a mistake, by the way. It alters your whole personality. What's happened to you? You seem to have changed completely . . .

Snell Snell. Kenneth Snell. Moore didn't come. They put me in his rooms.

Lady Driver *covers her eyes for some moments.*

Lady Driver Have you ever had the feeling that you'd like to get inside your handbag and close it firmly above your head? (*Puts the letter firmly away in her bag*) No, of course not – you haven't got a handbag. Where do men keep their things . . . ? Have you ever felt that you'd like to hide inside your trouser pocket . . . ? What *am* I talking about? I think it might be best

if I simply left without another word and went quietly to bed
with a cup of Ovaltine. Good night!

Snell   Oh, good night . . .

Lady Driver *exits to the stairs, and immediately enters again.*

Lady Driver   On second thoughts I'd like to stay and talk
for a moment. There are some people outside on the staircase,
and it would be nice to wait until they've gone. Is that very silly
of me? They seem to have had a certain amount to drink, and
they're falling about the stairs with a barrel. They're some
people I happen to know. I'd rather not embarrass them if I
can help it. There is a certain social barrier between the drunk
and the sober which is very difficult to bridge. *I* find. Especially
on a narrow staircase. And when they're all giggling helplessly.
And when they've got a barrel wedged on the turn of the stairs,
so that one would have to physically climb over them and the
barrel to get past. I don't know whether you think I'm being
a little over-sensitive about this?

Snell   You're the Master's wife, aren't you?

Lady Driver   Yes, well, that comes into it, of course.

Snell   I remember you from before. I used to see you
sometimes.

Lady Driver   Out of the window?

Snell   No – I didn't have a room in College. But sometimes
I'd come into College very early in the morning, before
breakfast, to have a bath. There was no bath in my lodgings,
you see. You used to climb out over that wall at the back of the
bath-house. That kind of thing wasn't possible in lodgings.

Lady Driver   I suppose not, if there was no bath. Well, I
must be on my way. I'm glad we met, finally, after all those
near misses on the bath-house roof. Would you just pop your
head outside the door for me and see if all the barrels and
bodies on the stairs have stopped happening?

Snell   I think they're coming up here, aren't they?

Lady Driver   Here?

Snell   I'll just look.

Snell *opens the door to look out, which happens to conceal* **Lady Driver** *behind it.* **Headingley** *and* **Buckle** *fall into the room with a beer barrel, followed by* **Tate** *holding tankards.*

Headingley   You're drunk, Buckle!

Buckle   *I'm* drunk?

Headingley   Drunk as a dormouse.

Buckle   You can't even stand up!

Headingley   Pissed as a coot.

Buckle   Look at you, rolling about the floor, you great tank of booze!

Headingley   You've shocked our bearded friend here.

Snell   No, no . . .

Buckle   He looks very worried about something.

Snell   I was just wondering if you ought to take all this stuff downstairs again.

Headingley   *What?*

Buckle   It's taken us all this time to get it upstairs!

Tate   Sh! Everyone's in bed! They're all trying to get to sleep!

Headingley   Close the door, then.

Tate *closes the door, revealing* **Lady Driver**. *Nobody sees her.*

Headingley   Just a moment, who have we got here? Are we all present? Someone's missing. You, me, you . . .

Taylor *enters, holding a banister, and the door conceals* **Lady Driver**.

Headingley   Bill. All right. That's better.

Taylor (*sternly*)   That *was* the original Jacobean banister, you know.

Buckle   Better off without it. We're doing our . . . What does your generation call it? We're doing our thing.

Headingley   Speak for yourself, you dirty bugger!

Tate   Oh, goodness me! Perhaps we'd better not have all this floating out for everyone to hear!

He closes the door, to prevent anyone outside hearing, and **Lady Driver** *appears.* **Snell** *becomes agitated.*

Buckle   Our bearded companion wants to take it downstairs again!

Snell   No, no. But . . . may I introduce . . . ?

Buckle (*ignores him*)   Hold on. Where are we going to put it?

Headingley   On the collapsible table.

Buckle   I bet it's absolute piss now. You've shaken it all up.

Headingley   It's you, you sod! How can you carry a barrel of beer and do your thing at the same time! It's not natural!

Buckle   God, you've got a filthy mind, Chris! I can't think how I can bring myself to associate with you.

Snell   Excuse me. I'd like you to meet . . .

Headingley   Just a moment. On the collapsible table . . .

They put the barrel on the collapsible table. It collapses. They collapse.

Buckle   It's collapsed!

Taylor   This furniture costs money, you know.

Headingley   I said, put it on the collapsible table!

Buckle   And it collapsed!

Snell   Excuse me. I don't know whether you know . . .

Quine *and* **Sainsbury** *enter, with two bottles of whisky, concealing* **Lady Driver**.

Headingley   Yes, yes.

Buckle   We know *them* all right.

Sainsbury   Oh, they're coming on nicely. They've reached giggling point.

Tate   Chris said, 'Put it on the collapsible table,' and it collapsed!

Taylor   Lot of people in the world who'd be glad of a table like that.

Buckle   Don't worry about the table, Bill.

Taylor   This isn't a holiday for some of us, you know.

Buckle   In the morning we'll all get together and make a most colossal contribution to the Organ Fund.

Headingley   There you go again! You've got a one-track mind!

Tate (*to* **Quine** *and* **Sainsbury**)   They're in form!

Sainsbury   It's funny – there's nothing that stops you laughing like the sight of other people laughing about something else.

Quine   Sing them a comic song, Dicky. One of those revue numbers that you and Roddy used to do. That'll wipe the smile off their faces.

Sainsbury   Shall I? Oh, how lovely! A humorous song from the shows of yesteryear. Shut the door, Alan.

Quine *shuts the door, and* **Lady Driver** *reappears.* **Snell** *makes a gesture of helpless fellow-feeling to her.* **Sainsbury** *pulls his jacket over his head, to simulate a nun's habit.*

Sainsbury (*parlando*)
    I'm a naughty old nun, in a nunnery!
    Yes, a funny old bun, in a nunnery!
    You might think life's dull in the cloister,
    That a cloister is nobody's oyster.
    But we've got a boister-
    Ous cloister – we roister!
    And some of our habits are dreadfully low!

He slips his jacket down off the shoulder, to form a low habit.
Headingley *and the others stop laughing.*

Sainsbury
Now, you know!
Oh, it's fun
Being a nun!
We can't kick the habit,
No, none of us!

Do you like it? It's called 'Nun the Less'.

Headingley   I can't think why we're sitting here listening to this rubbish.

Buckle   Why don't we sing our own dirty song?

Headingley   'The Odd Job Man!'

Buckle   'The Odd Job Man!'

Snell *hastily opens the door to conceal* **Lady Driver**.

Tate (*closes the door*)   No ladies around, I trust!

He nudges **Lady Driver**. *She smiles politely.*

Buckle   How does it go?

Sainsbury (*with a flourish between verses*)
With a hey and a ho and a hey nunny no . . . !

But at the sound of the other song he stops.

Headingley (*singing*)
The Duchess she called the Odd Job Man –

Buckle (*singing*)
She said, 'I've some odd jobs for you . . . '

Tate (*singing*)
'You can do them today
While his Grace is away . . . '

Headingley, Buckle *and* **Tate** (*together*)
'Little things he's neglected to do.'

Sainsbury
  With a hey and a ho and a hey nunny no . . . !

Headingley
  'Look under my skirting for mouseholes . . . '

Buckle
  'And ease off my drawers upstairs . . . '

Tate
  'I could do with a screw
  In the outside loo . . . '

Headingley, Buckle and **Tate** (*together*)
  'And stuffing in several armchairs.'

Snell *quietly opens the door, concealing* **Lady Driver**. **Taylor** *closes it, revealing her again.*

Sainsbury   Oh, for heaven's sake!

Headingley
  The Odd Job Man he said to the Duchess . . .

Buckle
  'To give satisfaction's my boast . . . '

Tate
  'I've done some odd jobs
  In my time for the nobs . . . '

Headingley, Buckle and **Tate** (*together*)
  'But this one is odder than most.'

Headingley   The Duchess she said to the Odd Job Man . . .

Buckle
  'I know when you're through you'll be feeling . . . '

Tate
  'Like a nice cup of tea –
  Well please! Allow me . . . !'

Headingley, Buckle and **Tate** (*together*)
  'Just give me a bang on the ceiling!'

They laugh and cheer. Their joviality evaporates as **Sainsbury** *resumes.*

Sainsbury (*firmly*)   Verse two. Striptease.

> I'm a naughty old nun with a history!
> Yes, a naughty old past wrapped in mystery!
> I first took the veil in Jerusalem,
> I liked it so much I took two of 'em!
> It was really quite heaven –
> I went on to take seven!
> Now I take them all off one by one for a pound,
> Dancing round,
> Very slow,
> Here we go . . . !

He begins to simulate a striptease.

Headingley   Come on, men! Debag him!

Snell *opens the door, concealing* **Lady Driver**, *as* **Sainsbury** *flees, pursued by* **Headingley**, **Buckle**, *and* **Tate**.

Sainsbury   The cloth! Respect the cloth! I'm a minister of religion!

Buckle   Off with his trousers!

Headingley   Off with his balls!

Tate   Those are his best trousers, you know . . .

Taylor   Mind the good banister! (*To* **Quine**.) What are they going to do? I'm responsible if anything happens. They're not going to paint slogans on anything, are they?

Quine   No, they're going to take Sainsbury's balls off.

Taylor (*out of the window*)   Yes, but not on the grass! Fellows only on the grass!

Quine   I'll lay evens. Evens on either ball. How about that? Three to one against the double.

Taylor   Get off him! (*To* **Quine**.) They're climbing up King Henry. You're supposed to be paying for the new building, not demolishing the old one.

He exits to the stairs. **Snell** *remains by the door.*

Quine   Why don't you go and join in the fun? Take a chamberpot with you.

Snell   No, no.

Quine   Come and sit down, then. Have a glass of whisky and tell me who you are. Shut the door.

Snell   You wouldn't prefer it open?

Quine   Why, do you have strong feelings about it?

Snell   No, no. No, no. I was just thinking . . .

Making up his mind, **Snell** *closes the door, revealing* **Lady Driver**.

Snell   May I introduce Lady Driver?

Lady Driver   Oh, we're old friends! Hello, Alan. I was just passing by, and I remembered you said something about dropping in for a drink . . . How was the dinner? Was the lamb all right? What did you think of the claret?

Quine (*gazes at her, then turns to* **Snell**)   Is this *your* guest?

Snell   No! Well . . . no.

Quine   It is, isn't it? You were concealing her.

Snell   No! Well . . . yes.

Quine   A lady in, after hours. That's a rather serious offence.

Snell   I don't think the rules apply to this lady, do they?

Quine   No, perhaps the rules don't apply to this lady. (*He laughs.*)

Snell   I mean, she's part of the College.

Quine   Part of the fixtures and fittings. (*Laughs.*)

Lady Driver   After tonight I never want to hear the sound of laughter again.

Quine   I'm sorry. I'll go. You two don't want me around.

Lady Driver   It's all very funny to you, isn't it? You're leaving tomorrow. I've got to go on living here! I've got to go on looking Bill Taylor and Sydney Birkett in the eye! Not to mention Harry! Harry and Christopher Headingley sit on committees together!

Quine   Is that your bicycle they're riding down there?

Lady Driver (*running to the window*)   Where?

Quine   The contents of the basket seem to have got scattered everywhere.

Lady Driver   My court files! My probation reports! (*She bursts into tears.*)

Snell   Oh dear. Oh dear, oh dear, oh dear. Come on, now. Cheer up. Don't worry.

Lady Driver   Oh, shut up!

Snell   Shall I pour her a drink? Or do you think we should just leave? How do you recommend coping with this kind of thing?

Quine   You go and collect up the papers.

Snell   The papers, yes.

Quine   And the bicycle. (*He closes the curtains meaningfully.*) I'll look after her.

Snell   Yes, well, I'm probably better at bicycles.

He exits to the stairs.

Quine (*gently, putting a consoling arm around* **Lady Driver**)   I don't think he's coming, is he? Never mind. Perhaps he will next time.

Lady Driver   Next time? In another twenty-five years?

Quine   Something to look forward to.

Lady Driver   I was going to be so calm and amused about it all.

Quine   Calm and amused? You?

Lady Driver   You don't know me these days.

Quine   You sit up there on the Bench, sending people down for fifteen years, being calm and amused?

Lady Driver   I've changed. I keep telling you.

Quine   I'll tell you what you do. You leave your wig behind. You put the photographs of the body in your bag and get them mixed up with old love letters from prosecuting counsel.

Lady Driver   I don't wear a wig. I'm a magistrate, not a judge.

Sainsbury *enters. His collar is missing.* **Lady Driver** *hides her face in* **Quine***'s chest.*

Sainsbury   It's their aim that terrifies me! It was my *trousers* they were trying to . . . (*He sees* **Lady Driver**.) Alan! I don't believe it!

Quine   Good night, Dicky.

Sainsbury   I'd turn my back on you for two minutes in the old days, at the most improbable party, and you'd have conjured some girl out of the air. But here! Now! This verges on the uncanny!

Quine   Good night.

Sainsbury   Well . . . good night. Sleep well. See you in breakfast. Perhaps. If you need the services of a minister of religion at any point, I think you'll probably find me in the river.

He exits.

Lady Driver   Alan, will you please get me out of here before anyone else comes in?

Quine   We'll go across the landing to my room. You'll be perfectly safe there.

Lady Driver   That's very hospitable of you, but I think I'll be safer still if you'd see me back to the Master's Lodge. Has everything stopped happening outside . . . ?

She parts the curtains and looks out of the window. **Sainsbury** *enters, pursued by* **Headingley**, **Buckle**, **Tate** *and* **Taylor**.

Sainsbury   No! Pax!

Headingley   We'll defenestrate him!

Taylor   Please open the window first.

Sainsbury   No! Stop! Fainites! Put me down! I'll excommunicate you! Listen, listen! You can't come in here! Look! Look! Look!

He at last persuades them to look at what he is pointing at – **Lady Driver**'s *legs, visible below the bottom of the curtain. Silence. They all turn to look at* **Quine**. *They turn back to look at the legs. First one leg, then the other, discreetly vanishes, as* **Lady Driver**, *behind the curtain, steps up on to the window seat to hide herself completely.*

Buckle   Good God!

Headingley   A woman!

Tate   A lady!

Buckle   A popsy!

Taylor   A female!

Tate   Oh, sizzling sausages!

Quine *opens the door to the stairs, and waits for them to go. They are all shaken and sobered. They keep their voices down.*

Buckle   I have to say, I find it a little unsavoury.

Headingley   At an occasion of this nature.

Tate   In College.

Taylor   At your time of life.

Sainsbury   It makes the rest of us look so uncommonly foolish.

They troop out. **Lady Driver** *begins to emerge from the curtains. They burst back into the room. She vanishes again.*

Headingley   But . . . where did you *find* her?

Tate   There's something going on somewhere!

Buckle   A party. One of the language schools giving a dance.

Headingley   Because if there *is* something going on, we might as well all join in the fun.

Buckle   Come on, Alan, where is it?

Quine   Just across the street. I'll show you.

Taylor   You can't get out. The College is locked up for the night, owing to industrial action.

Headingley   Where are the keys?

Taylor   That's what *I'd* like to know.

Tate   Who's got them?

Buckle   Where did we put them?

They pat their pockets.

Quine   You'll have to climb out.

Tate   Oh, gooseberries! Climbing out!

Headingley   Come on, chaps! Who's game?

Buckle   Over the bath-house roof!

Tate   Oh, great jumping jellies!

Quine (*ushering* **Headingley** *towards the stairs*)   Minister . . .

Headingley   No! Lead the way!

Quine *exits, noisily followed by* **Buckle** *and* **Tate***, then* **Sainsbury**. **Taylor** *follows them.*

Taylor   The College accepts no responsibility for personal injury!

Headingley *is about to follow them, then hesitates. He looks out to the staircase to make sure that the others have gone.* **Lady Driver** *opens the* *curtain, sees* **Headingley** *looking out of the door, and hastily closes the curtains again as he turns back to look in her direction. He closes the door and walks quietly across to the window. He looks round once again to make sure he is unobserved, then bends down to look up under the curtains. Pause.* **Lady Driver***'s head emerges cautiously from the top of them, trying to see what's going on below.*

Snell *enters from the stairs with an armful of files.*

Snell   Files!

Lady Driver *disappears instantly.* **Headingley** *springs to his feet, clutches his back with a cry of pain, and doubles up again.*

Snell   Sorry! Sorry! I didn't meant to startle you!

Headingley *tries to straighten up again, with the same result.*

Snell   Wait there, wait there. I'll fetch someone . . . I've never lived through a night like this!

He exits. **Headingley** *very slowly and cautiously straightens up, holding on to the curtains for support, and is hit by the same spasm of pain as before. He doubles up, bringing the curtains down with him, and revealing* **Lady Driver**.

Lady Driver (*sociably*)   Christopher!

Headingley (*springs upright*)   Rosemary! (*He doubles up again, straightens, and doubles, as if he is bowing before an altar.*)

Lady Driver   I think you said something about looking in for a drink after dinner, didn't you? (*Gets down from the window seat.*) I know there were various points Harry wanted to take up with you about the future of the University Grants Committee . . .

Headingley *makes a further unsuccessful attempt to rise.*

Lady Driver   You have a back, do you?

Headingley   No.

Lady Driver   I think perhaps you have one now.

Headingley *cries out again.*

Lady Driver   You can't stay like that all night, Christopher. You'll just have to be very brave and jump up straight, won't you?

Headingley *is very brave, and jumps up straight, and sinks to his knees with a roar of pain, clutching his back and* **Lady Driver**. **Quine** *and* **Snell** *enter.*

Lady Driver   His back.

Quine   I can see he is. And proposing to you.

Snell   I never realised what living in College involved.

Tate *enters, followed by* **Buckle** *and* **Taylor**.

Tate   Did someone scream . . . ?

He stops short at the sight of **Lady Driver**, *who has turned aside to conceal her face.*

Tate   Oh, great sainted lollipops – he's found one already!

Buckle   What?

Taylor   What?

Tate   He's found one!

Buckle   *Found* one . . . ? Good God!

Tate (*pushes* **Buckle** *out of the room*)   We'd better leave them to it . . . I say, Chris, well done!

Tate *and* **Buckle** *exit.* **Taylor** *remains.*

Taylor (*puzzled*)   Rosemary . . . ?

Lady Driver   Oh, hello, Bill. Do you know Christopher Headingley?

Quine   Parliamentary Under-Secretary of State at the Department of Education?

Taylor   But, Rosemary, I don't understand what you're doing *here.* You were supposed to be downstairs in *my* rooms. Remember? We were going to go into overtime together. You were going to knock me down and walk all over me.

Lady Driver   Thank you, Bill, for those few well-chosen words. They set the seal on a memorable evening. On that note I think I shall leave. Thank you, Christopher. Thank you, Alan.

Quine   I'll see you back.

Lady Driver   No, no. I'll just slip quietly away without another word and look for an all-night nunnery to enter. Good night!

She exits to the stairs.

Taylor   Something *I* said?

Snell   Strange creatures, women. I find. Don't you? Do you find them strange, in your experience?

Taylor   What?

Snell   Sit down, sit down. (*To* **Headingley**.) Can you manage to sit down now? We'll all have a drink. The night is young. I shall be most interested to hear everyone's views on women. What can I put the whisky in? A tooth-glass! Whisky out of a tooth-glass! My God! What next?

He exits to the bedroom with one of the bottles of whisky.

Quine   I think at our age we have to find less violent sports, don't we, Minister?

Headingley   What I can't remember is what we were doing in this room in the first place.

Quine   Waiting for Roddy.

Headingley   Oh yes. Where the hell is he?

Quine   Stood us all up.

Headingley   Just like Roddy.

Quine   Doesn't know what he's missing, does he?

Taylor   Never mind. We'll send him a banker's order form.

Quine   Well, that's about the end of the evening, isn't it? We'll give you a hand downstairs.

He helps **Headingley** *to his feet, and assists him to the door. He is still curiously bent, unable to stand straight.* **Headingley**, **Quine** *and* **Taylor** *exit to the stairs with the second bottle of whisky.* **Snell** *enters from the bedroom, pouring whisky into a tooth-glass.*

Snell   Because my trouble is this: I refuse to compromise. I demand the perfect woman . . . ! Is that the right amount? No, that's too much . . . *(He pours some back.)* Now, am I being unrealistic? Tell me frankly, because what I've always missed is a chance like this to really talk about life . . . *(He sees that he is talking to himself.)* Ah. *(Bitterly.)* Of course! *(He looks at the tumbler of whisky, fills it to the brim, and lifts it to drink.)*

Lady Driver *enters from the stairs.*

Lady Driver   Some fool has locked up the Master's Lodge. I'm very sorry, but I'm going to have to spend the night in your armchair. *(She sits.)* Good night. Don't let me keep you up.

Snell *looks at her. Then he carefully sets down the bottle of whisky; walks to the door holding his brimming tooth-glass; locks the door; turns his back on* **Lady Driver**; *drinks down the whisky and flings down the glass; turns back to face her; smoothes his hair; gives a great roaring gasp as the whisky catches up with him; and staggers wildly towards her. She leaps out of the chair and hides behind it.*

Curtain.

Act Two

Headingley's *rooms. Day.*

Two doors, one to the stairs, one to the bedroom, and a window, much as in **Snell**'s *room.*

A bell is tolling, off. **Headingley** *enters from the bedroom, in pyjamas, holding his head in one hand and the trousers he was wearing when he arrived in the other. He moves slowly and carefully, intent upon inward sensations. He stands looking around for something. The bell stops, and he discovers the trousers in his hand. He begins to put them on, then realises that he is still wearing his pyjama trousers. He bends down to disentangle his feet and take them off again.*

A discreet tap at the door to the stairs.

Headingley Come in.

Pause. He struggles slowly with the trousers. Another tap, a little louder.

(*Impatiently.*) Come in! (*He automatically straightens up – and doubles over again with a cry of pain, holding his back.*)

Buckle *enters, dressed in weekend clothes, and holding an aerosol of shaving foam. He is also moving slowly and carefully.*

Buckle Oh. You're back.

Headingley *slowly straightens himself.*

Headingley Nothing. Just a . . . Agh!

Buckle I mean, in your rooms. (*He indicates.*) I thought you might still be . . . upstairs.

Headingley Upstairs?

Buckle In Roddy's rooms. Last night. Where you were.

Headingley No.

He makes another cautious attempt to descend to trouser level, but is forced to give up.

Buckle   You feeling . . . ?

Headingley   Fine.

Buckle   A bit . . . ?

Headingley   A bit.

Buckle   Yes, I feel a bit . . . Nothing serious. Just a shade.

Headingley   Exactly.

Buckle (*gazes at* **Headingley***'s feet*)   Pyjamas.

Headingley   Yes.

Buckle   Still on.

Headingley   Yes. (*He doesn't move.*)

Buckle   Feel like breakfast?

Headingley   No.

Buckle   No.

He turns to leave, then remembers the shaving foam.

Oh, found this outside. Thought it might be yours. Shaving foam.

He gives it to **Headingley**, *who gazes at it blankly.*

Buckle   Spraying it around a bit. Last night. King Henry, and so on. White moustache. Weren't we?

Headingley   Were we?

Tate *enters from the stairs, dressed and cheerful. He bangs on the open door. They flinch.*

Tate   Who's for eggs and bacon? Hello, Chris! Hello, David! I say, what a super morning! We really have picked the right weekend for it, you know. Sun streaming into chapel this morning! But only three of us there! Isn't that awful? You two both look in good form, though.

Headingley   Fine.

Buckle   Fine.

Tate   I feel as fresh as a daisy. But then I finished up with a nice bracing dip in the river. They threw me in the river, Chris!

Buckle *(dimly recalls)*   Oh yes.

Tate   Oh yes, he says!

Buckle   Sorry about that.

Tate   No, it cleared my head.

Buckle   Not getting at you personally.

Tate   Oh, I took it all in good part. I usually take my clothes off first, so it made a change!

Buckle   I think we just felt it would . . . round the evening off. Didn't we?

Headingley   Did we?

Tate   Oh, *Chris* wasn't there . . . *(He becomes aware of* **Headingley**'s *state of dress.)* Chris . . . Pyjamas. Still on.

Headingley *makes another unsuccessful attempt to bend down.*

Tate   No, this was after you'd moved on to higher things! If one might put it like that! *(He discovers* **Headingley**'s *evening clothes, lying in a crumpled heap.)* Oh dear, your poor old dinner jacket! Thrown down in the heat of the moment! *(He picks up the things and folds them.)* I do take my hat off, though! Rather reassuring to know that some of us can still show the youngsters a thing or two! Anyway, all over and forgotten now. Back to the straight and narrow for another twenty-five years! *(He takes the things towards the bedroom.)* I'll just hang these up for you . . . *(He stops.)* Oh, is it all right to go in? *(Puts* **Headingley**'s *evening shoes down by the bedroom door, and everything else over* **Headingley**'s *arm.)* Just to be on the safe side. Don't want to cause any red faces! Well, I don't know about you two, but I'm starving! How about a spot of breakfast?

Buckle   Not just at the moment. Thank you, Norman.

Tate   No? Well, I'll see you later, then. Mm! I can smell those kippers grilling from here!

He exits to the stairs.

Buckle (*keeping his voice down*)   She's *not* still in there, is she?

Headingley   What *is* all this?

Buckle   The lady.

Headingley   What lady?

Buckle   Last night.

Headingley (*understands*)   Oh . . . !

Buckle   We were fearfully impressed. Shocked. But impressed.

Headingley   No, no. Just a friend of mine.

Buckle   Staggering.

Headingley   No, no.

Buckle   Real old-fashioned craftsmanship.

Headingley   Not at all. Simply a friend. Old friend. Someone I hadn't seen for some time. Norman thought it was . . . ?

Buckle   Staggering.

Headingley   No, just an old friend looking in for a chat.

He waddles off into the bedroom with the evening clothes, still holding the shaving foam.

Buckle   Well, as long as Norman doesn't do anything silly. Didn't he say he wrote things in the newspapers?

A moment – then **Headingley** *enters, suddenly awake and anxious. His trousers are still round his ankles, and he is still holding the shaving foam. But he has put the evening clothes down, and is holding a toothbrush.*

Headingley   Wrote things? In the newspapers?

Buckle   Oh, I don't think he *would*, though. Not about a member of the same college. Anyway, no one would print that sort of thing . . . Very few papers would print that sort of thing . . . I'm sure he realises that with a man in your position this is exactly the kind of thing that some people are on the lookout for.

Headingley   Can you catch him before he goes? Explain to him it was just an old friend?

Buckle (*doesn't believe him*)   An old friend. Right . . .

Headingley   I'm not dressed.

Buckle   No . . .

Headingley   Well, then, fetch him along here. *I'll* tell him.

Buckle   I think you politicians are better equipped to handle this kind of thing.

Buckle *exits to the stairs*

Headingley *looks abstractedly at the toothbrush and the shaving foam, trying to remember what he is doing with them. He is about to spray foam onto the toothbrush when he is distracted by a sharp knock on the door.*
Snell *enters. He is wearing his dinner jacket still, but his bow tie and his shirt cuffs are undone, and his manner has completely changed.*

Snell   I want a mature studentship.

Headingley   What?

Snell   A mature studentship.

Headingley   A mature studentship?

Snell   A mature studentship, as I understand it, is intended for applicants of mature years who missed their educational opportunities when they were younger.

Headingley   Dinner jacket . . .

Snell   I missed my educational opportunities when I was younger. I see that now. I'd like to come into residence this October. I don't want to waste any more time.

Headingley   Haven't you been to bed?

Snell   I'm ready to take the College entrance exam again if they want me to. But that is a concession. I have a *right* to a room in College. I had a right to a room in College in my third year and I was cheated out of it.

Headingley   Yes. Well, you must talk to the College about that.

Snell   I haven't been to sleep all night. I've been walking up and down, thinking about this.

Headingley   Not me. Nothing to do with me.

Snell   I'm keeping the rooms! You won't catch me that way again! Of course, I realise that's not the province of the Department of Education.

Headingley   No, the College.

Snell   I don't blame the Department of Education for what happened before.

Headingley   The College, the College.

Snell   The College, exactly. And as for having a girl in my rooms all night . . . ! What? Out beyond the station? Don't make me laugh!

Headingley   See Dr Taylor.

Snell   I wasted my time here! That's the tragedy. I just worked, and worked, and cycled back and forth to my lodgings, and got a second.

Headingley   Across the landing.

Snell   I never wore a fancy waistcoat.

Headingley   Dr Taylor.

Snell   I never wrote a blasphemous poem. I never had a bath in a women's college.

Headingley   Get the forms from Dr Taylor.

Snell   I wasn't ready for it, you see. That was the thing.
I didn't know the trick, I hadn't got the knack. I wasn't old
enough to be young. But now I could do it! Do you see?
Because here I am, doing it! Do you see that? I am making
sense, aren't I? I mean, here I am! Rooms in College! Girl in
all night! No trouble! Easiest thing in the world – now!

Headingley   Put it in writing.

Snell   I'm going out to buy the Sunday papers. Then we'll sit
on the floor all morning, drinking coffee and reading the papers.
I know the things you do, all right! And now I can do them!
It's as simple as that! Dr Taylor?

Headingley   Dr Taylor.

Snell   Bill Taylor?

Headingley   Bill Taylor.

Snell   He'd be the man to talk to, would he?

Headingley   Yes, he would.

Snell   I'll get the papers. Then I'll talk to Bill.

Headingley   Right.

Snell   Good move to come and see you first, though.

Headingley   Of course.

Snell   Start at the top. Pull any strings you can. Seize your
chances. That's the lesson I've learnt.

Headingley   Good.

Snell   I think it's been a valuable talk.

Headingley   I think so.

Snell   For me, at any rate. Clarified my ideas.

Headingley   That's the way.

Snell   I wish I could tell you how simple everything seems to
me now.

Headingley   Tell Bill Taylor.

Snell   And I've got my bicycle with me, so the whole arrangement is very convenient. Bill Taylor?

Headingley   Bill Taylor.

Snell *exits.*

Headingley *thoughtfully sprays shaving foam on to his toothbrush. He bares his teeth, then looks at the brush and stops, thinks, and brushes the shaving foam onto his face.*

Lady Driver *rushes in, leaving the door open, and wearing the suit in which* **Quine** *arrived the previous afternoon. She is still wearing her own shoes and clutching her bag.*

Lady Driver   A newspaper!

Headingley   Rosemary . . . ?

Lady Driver   A newspaper!

Headingley   A newspaper?

Lady Driver   A *newspaper*!

Headingley (*alarmed*)   A *newspaper*?

He drags his trousers up, agony or no agony, over his pyjamas.

Where?

Lady Driver   Where?

Headingley   Here?

He closes the door to the stairs.

Lady Driver   There?

Headingley   Which one?

Lady Driver   Which what?

Headingley   Which newspaper?

Lady Driver   *Which* newspaper? I don't mind *which* newspaper! *Any* newspaper!

Headingley   *Any* newspaper?

Lady Driver   Look, have you got a newspaper, or haven't you?

Headingley   Just a moment. Let me get this clear. Is there or is there not a newspaper snooping around here?

Lady Driver   I can't understand what you're talking about. I simply want a newspaper!

Headingley   You *want* a newspaper?

Lady Driver   I *want* a newspaper.

Headingley   Rosemary, what do you want a newspaper *for*?

Lady Driver   What do I want a newspaper *for*? I want a newspaper to *read*!

Headingley   To *read*?

Lady Driver   Oh for heaven's *sake*!

Headingley   Has something happened? Not the Government? Not Education?

Lady Driver   I want a newspaper to read while I'm walking back to the Master's Lodge! So that it's in front of my face! I can't walk through the College in broad daylight with this face sticking out of Alan Quine's suit! Birkett's back on duty! You can't run a College like that!

Headingley   But, Rosemary . . . Why are you wearing Alan Quine's suit?

Lady Driver   Because that lunatic with a beard is having a breakdown!

Headingley   I know, but . . .

Lady Driver   He's been walking up and down all night, talking to himself! He wouldn't let me out! He wants me to get a divorce! He wants us to get married in the Chapel! Then he went out this morning and locked me in!

Headingley   Nevertheless . . .

Lady Driver   So I had to get out through the window! And into Alan Quine's room!

Headingley (*gestures at the suit*)   But Rosemary, Rosemary, why . . . ?

Lady Driver   Because half my dress is now on the spikes! The Master's wife can't walk through College on Sunday morning in half a dress! Colleges aren't organised on that basis! As a junior Minister of Education might be expected to realise!

Headingley   But doesn't Alan Quine want to wear his . . . ?

Lady Driver   No! He's asleep! Like you!

Headingley   Rosemary . . .

Lady Driver   I'm living through a nightmare! I expect my friends to help!

Headingley   I don't know where to start.

Lady Driver   With a newspaper.

Headingley   I haven't *got* a newspaper!

Lady Driver   All that, and he hasn't got a newspaper.

Headingley   Bill Taylor.

Lady Driver   A Government minister, and he hasn't got a newspaper.

Headingley   Try Bill Taylor.

Lady Driver   How you became a politician, Christopher, I shall never know!

She exits, slamming the door. She reappears immediately.

People!

Headingley   The paper *The People*?

A knock at the door.

Buckle (*off*)   Chris? It's David. I've got Norman with me.

Headingley (*groans*)   Oh. *Those* people.

Lady Driver   Here we go again.

She prepares to hide behind the door once more.

Headingley (*indicating the bedroom*)   In here!

Lady Driver   Bedroom? No!

Headingley   Yes!

Lady Driver   I won't!

Headingley   You must!

Buckle (*off*)   Chris? Are you there?

Headingley (*to* **Buckle**)   Coming! (*To* **Lady Driver**.)
Newspapers!

Lady Driver   Newspapers?

Headingley   Norman Tate.

Lady Driver   He's got them?

Headingley   He is them. Not just my career.

Lady Driver   No, *my* career.

Headingley   Entire Government.

Lady Driver   Good riddance.

Headingley   Whole economy!

Lady Driver   Oh, the economy.

Buckle (*off*)   Chris, what's happening?

Headingley   Won't forget this.

Lady Driver   Nor shall I.

She exits to the bedroom. **Buckle** *and* **Tate** *enter from the stairs.*

Buckle   What are you up to?

Headingley   Nothing.

Tate   We thought you must have gone back to bed!

Headingley   Bed? No, no.

Tate   No, I can see, you were shaving.

Headingley   No, no. (*He lets go his trousers to feel his chin and finds lather on his fingers.*) Yes, I was shaving.

Buckle   Well, carry on.

Tate   Don't let us disturb you.

Headingley   No, nice to down tools for a moment.

Buckle   We only looked in for a chat. Didn't we, Norman?

Tate   Shave away, Chris.

Headingley   Sit down. So, you looked in for a chat.

Tate   Where's the razor? In here?

He starts to open the bedroom door.

Headingley   *Sit down!* If we're going to chat, let's chat.

Tate   Oh. Sorry.

Buckle   The thing is this. I was just nattering away over breakfast with our friend Norman here about the events of last night. And it transpired that he had rather leapt to conclusions. If one might put it like that.

Tate   I thought it was staggering.

Buckle   He thought it was staggering. So I said, no, no, as I understood it, it wasn't staggering at all, it was simply an old friend of yours who happened to drop by at that particular moment of time.

Tate   At which I just *laughed*!

Buckle   At which he just *laughed*. So I said, well, let's not make a great issue of this, but why don't we stroll round to Christopher's rooms when you've finished your toast and marmalade, and get the whole thing straight from the horse's mouth?

Headingley Well, I'm glad you did. Because it does show you how easily a rumour of this sort can start. If only newspapers always took the trouble to check their information in this very sensible way, they wouldn't find themselves faced with cripplingly expensive libel actions.

Tate Chris, sorry, but I can't bear to see you sitting there with lather all over your, face. I'll get you a towel.

He opens the bedroom door again.

Headingley I have a towel! Here . . . (*He wipes his face on the curtain.*) No, as I was saying, it's very easy to get hold of the wrong end of the stick . . .

Quine *enters, in pyjamas.*

Quine (*to* **Headingley**) It was *you*, wasn't it?

Headingley (*groans*) *Now* what?

Quine All part of the fun and games, I suppose.

Headingley What *is* everyone on about this morning?

Quine I thought we'd got all the japes and jollity over last night. Where is it?

Headingley Where's *what*?

Quine My suit.

Headingley (*realises*) Oh, your suit.

Quine I thought so. In here?

He tries to enter the bedroom.

Headingley (*prevents him*) Get away from that door!

Quine Take your hands off me!

Headingley Take *your* hands off my door handle!

Quine Look, I'm not going to be pushed around by some pisspot junior minister!

Headingley And I'm not having some greasy little civil servant snooping round my bedroom!

They fight – groggily, ineffectually, in slow motion.

Tate   Oh, dolloping doughnuts!

Buckle (*trying to separate the combatants*)   Now, calm down, Alan. Take it easy, Chris. We're not up to this kind of thing this morning. Somebody's going to get hurt . . . Ugh!

He turns away, holding his eye.

Tate   Stop! Stop! David's got a cut eye!

Headingley *and* **Quine** *stop.*

Tate   We can soon settle this. *I'll* look. (*He opens the bedroom door.*)

Headingley   *Bill Taylor!*

Tate *stops.*

Headingley   Bill Taylor's got the suit!

Quine   Bill Taylor?

Headingley   I saw him! Running round the bath-house with it!

Quine   Bill Taylor . . .

He exits to the stairs.

Headingley   Quick! Run after him! Help him! Stop him!

Buckle *exits after* **Quine**, *holding his eye.* **Tate** *turns back towards the bedroom.*

Headingley   Where do you think *you're* going?

Tate   Cold flannel. For David's eye.

Headingley   Bill Taylor! Bill Taylor's got a cold flannel!

Tate *exits to the stairs.* **Headingley** *closes the stairs door and opens the bedroom door.*

Headingley   Suit!

Lady Driver *enters from the bedroom.*

Lady Driver   Suit?

Headingley   Suit! Suit! Suit!

Lady Driver   What do you mean, Suit, suit, suit?

Headingley   Take it off!

Lady Driver   Take it off?

Headingley   Take it off! Alan Quine! He's awake! He's coming back!

The stairs door opens.

Here he is!

He bundles **Lady Driver** *back into the bedroom.* **Snell** *enters, carrying newspapers.*

Snell   Where is she? I left her behind *locked doors*! In *my* rooms! Rooms that are mine *by right*!

Headingley   Bill Taylor.

Snell   What are you lot trying to do to me? Destroy my life?

Headingley   Bill Taylor.

Snell   Taking something out of someone's rooms – that's stealing.

Headingley   Bill Taylor.

Snell *dumps the newspapers and goes towards the bedroom.*

Snell   She's in here, isn't she? Things have changed, you know! You lot aren't going to go on wiping your boots on me!

Headingley   She's in Bill Taylor's rooms!

Snell   I've just been in Bill Taylor's rooms.

Headingley   Yes – sorry . . . In Quine's rooms.

Snell (*stopping*)   In *Quine's* rooms?

Headingley   Quine. Upstairs. Quine.

Snell   It's one of you lot, I know that.

Headingley   Yes, Quine.

Snell   Quine. That's plausible. But if she's not with Quine I'll be back. You know I'm a Fifth Dan?

He snatches off one shoe and does his martial arts kick. **Headingley** *flinches back.* **Snell** *exits to the stairs, still holding his shoe.*
Headingley *closes the stairs door and opens the bedroom door.*

Headingley   Run!

Lady Driver *enters from the bedroom, wrapped in a bedsheet, without her handbag.*

Lady Driver   Run?

Headingley   Man with beard.

Lady Driver   Where?

Headingley   Here.

Lady Driver   Gone?

Headingley   Coming back.

Lady Driver   He's mad!

Headingley   So run!

Lady Driver *runs to the stairs door, then stops.*

Lady Driver   Sheet.

Headingley   Sheet?

Lady Driver   You said!

Headingley   I didn't say sheet!

Lady Driver   You said suit!

Headingley   I said run!

Lady Driver   God, politicians! (*She exits to the stairs, and immediately reappears.*) Quine!

Headingley   Quine?

Lady Driver   Coming here!

Headingley   Suit!

Lady Driver   You *want* the suit?

Headingley   Suit, suit, suit, suit, suit, suit, suit!

Lady Driver *exits into the bedroom.* **Quine**, **Buckle** *and* **Tate** *enter from the stairs.* **Buckle** *is holding a flannel to his eye.*

Quine   *Not* in Bill Taylor's rooms!

Tate   We ransacked them!

Headingley   Man with the beard!

Buckle   Bill was a bit cross about it.

Headingley   Man with the beard!

Buckle   We found a flannel.

Quine   But no suit!

Headingley   Beard! Beard! Beard!

Quine   Beard?

Headingley   Rushed in here. Suit. Papers. Threw down the papers.

He shows the newspapers that **Snell** *left.*

Quine   I'll murder him!

He exits to the stairs.

Tate   Poor little man!

Buckle   Stop him! Stop him!

He and **Tate** *exit after* **Quine**. **Headingley** *closes the stairs door.* **Lady Driver** *enters from the bedroom, wrapped in the bedsheet still and holding the suit.*

Lady Driver   Suit!

Headingley   Suit . . . (*He takes it, exits to the stairs with it, and immediately reappears.*) Man with the beard!

Lady Driver   Man with the beard . . .

She exits into the bedroom. **Snell** *enters from the stairs, still with one shoe on and one shoe off.*

Snell   *Not* in Quine's rooms!

Headingley   Isn't she?

Snell   No!

Headingley   No – because she's in *your* rooms!

Snell   In *my* rooms?

Headingley   With Quine!

Snell   With Quine?

Headingley   Rushed in here. Tore his suit off.

He shows the suit.

Snell   Took his *clothes* off?

Headingley   Rushed upstairs.

Snell   To *my* rooms?

Headingley   To *your* rooms.

Snell   I'll kick his face in!

He kicks to demonstrate. **Headingley** *flinches.*

Headingley   Suit! Give him his suit!

But **Snell** *has already gone. The bedroom door opens.*

Lady Driver (*off*)   Shoes!

Headingley *runs back to the bedroom door.*

Headingley (*to* **Lady Driver**)   Wait! (*To* **Snell**.) Come back!

Lady Driver (*off*)   Shoes!

Headingley (*to* **Lady Driver**)   Don't move! (*To* **Snell**.) Suit!

Lady Driver (*off*)   Shoes!

Headingley (*to* **Lady Driver**, *in explanation*)   Get rid of it!

He runs out after **Snell** *as* **Lady Driver** *enters from the bedroom, in* **Headingley**'s *evening clothes, barefoot, shirt cuffs and bow tie flapping, her bag on her arm, holding her own shoes.*

Lady Driver   Shoes! Shoes! Where are your *shoes*? (*Shows her own shoes in explanation.*) High heels! Dinner jacket! (*Sees* **Headingley**'s *evening shoes.*) Shoes . . .

She throws her own shoes back into the bedroom and picks up **Headingley**'s *shoes. Runs towards the door, then finds the handbag on her arm and hesitates, holding it against the dinner jacket.*

Lady Driver   Bag!

She runs back and throws the bag into the bedroom after the shoes. Runs towards the door, dragging on one of the shoes as she goes.

Taylor *enters, in his pyjamas, a hand shading his eyes from the brutal light of day.*

Taylor   Look, I didn't know this was a two-day festival.

Lady Driver, *one shoe on and one shoe off, diverts from the door, grabs one of the Sunday papers that* **Snell** *left behind, and opens it in front of her face, as if reading it, as* **Taylor** *takes his hand away from his eyes.*

Taylor   I've already had three hooligans bursting into my rooms this morning and turning everything over. Not to mention some screaming lunatic still wearing his dinner jacket. Tore his shoe off and lashed out at me with his . . .

He notices **Lady Driver**'s *trousers and single shoe beneath the newspaper, and her flapping shirt cuffs on either side of it.*

Taylor   . . . bare foot.

Headingley *enters from the stairs without the suit.*

Headingley (*to* **Taylor**)   Oh, you as well?

Taylor (*indicating* **Lady Driver**)   Watch out for this fellow with the beard.

Headingley   And *him* again?

Taylor   He woke me up this morning to tell me he wants a mature studentship.

Headingley   Yes. Give him one.

Taylor   Give him one?

Headingley   Give him a mature studentship, if that's what he wants!

Taylor   I can't just hand out mature studentships! What – on Sunday morning? In my pyjamas?

Headingley   Well, get him out of here!

Taylor   How? He's berserk!

They look at **Lady Driver**.

Taylor   He *was* berserk.

Headingley   He's gone quiet.

Taylor   There's something funny about the way he's reading that paper.

Buckle *enters, still with the flannel to his eye.*

Buckle   That man with the beard . . .

Tate *enters.*

Tate   . . . rushed in . . .

Buckle   . . . in his dinner jacket . . .

Quine *hobbles in, doubled over.*

Tate   . . . and kicked Alan in the wee-wee!

Buckle   He's plainly in the middle of a gross psychotic breakdown.

They see that **Headingley** *is silently indicating* **Lady Driver**.

Tate   Oh, hedgehogs!

Buckle   Now look at him.

Quine   Reading the business news.

Buckle   Leave this to me.

Tate   Thank heavens we've got a doctor here!

Quine   You can sew his balls back on!

He kicks at **Lady Driver**'*s newspaper, but is restrained by* **Buckle**.

Buckle   Calm down, Alan. Nothing to get worked up about. Simple medical problem. Norman, will you run and have a word with Mr Birkett? Ask him to ring for an ambulance.

Tate   Ambulance. Right. (*He exits.*)

Buckle (*to* **Lady Driver**)   Come along, then, old chap. Let's have a look at you.

Taylor   Careful, he may suddenly flare up again.

Buckle   Leave it to me, will you, Bill? I can still see out of one eye.

Quine   Keep away from his foot.

Headingley   You know he's a Fifth Dan?

Buckle (*to* **Headingley** *and* **Quine**)   Would you mind? (*To* **Lady Driver**.) Let's put the newspaper down, shall we? We'll have plenty of time for a jolly good read later on.

He tries to take the paper. **Lady Driver** *screams and kicks out.* **Buckle** *jumps back in alarm.* **Lady Driver** *pulls the paper over her head and runs towards the bedroom, still with one bare foot.*

Headingley (*blocking her way*)   Not in the bedroom!

Lady Driver *turns and advances slowly towards the staircase door instead. They retreat in front of her.*

Buckle   He's going.

Quine   Don't just stand there! Stop him!

Lady Driver *suddenly makes a run for it, and they all jump back. She exits to the stairs.*

Headingley   Run after him! Run, run!

Quine *exits.*

Headingley (*to* **Taylor**)   Come on! Before he damages College property!

Taylor   If I'd known everyone was going to get up this morning and start running round with paper bags over their heads . . .

He exits.

Headingley (*to* **Buckle**)   Quick! Before he kills someone!

Buckle   Keep calm! I've got my medical bag in the car. It's just a question of patience and understanding and fifty milligrams of Valium.

He exits. **Headingley** *closes the stairs door behind him and runs to the bedroom door.*

Headingley   Out!

Nothing happens.

Move, move!

The staircase door opens.

Don't move!

He closes the bedroom door. **Tate** *enters.*

Tate   Can you see him out of the window?

He runs to an invisible downstage window to look. **Taylor** *enters and runs to the window.*

Taylor   He ran straight towards the Master's Lodge!

Tate   Birkett chased him off with the bung-hammer!

Taylor   And he shot up the fire escape!

Tate   Onto the chapel!

Quine *hobbles in, and joins them at the window.*

Quine   I nearly got him with that bottle.

Headingley   Outside, outside. Watch it all outside.

He holds the staircase door open for them. They ignore him.

Taylor   There he is!

They all gaze upwards. Pause.

Tate   Is that parapet safe?

Pause. They all catch their breath and look away, then look back.

Taylor   He's not going to throw himself off, is he?

Headingley   Get out there! Hold out a sheet!

Sainsbury enters, wearing a suit but collarless.

Sainsbury   You haven't by any chance seen a clerical collar lying around, have you? Size seven. I can't go into Chapel like this.

Tate   Dicky! Dicky!

He silently indicates the scene outside.

Sainsbury   What? (*He looks.*)

Taylor   Talk to him! Talk him down!

Tate   You're a clergyman!

Sainsbury gazes, trying to understand.

Quine   It's the man with the beard.

Tate   He's having a bit of a crisis.

Quine   He's stolen my suit.

Tate   Go on, Dicky!

Headingley   But outside, yes? Outside!

Sainsbury   Oh dear . . . I wish I'd got my collar on.

Taylor   Get on with it!

Sainsbury   You haven't seen it, have you?

Quine   He'll be off there before you've started!

Sainsbury (*calling out of the window*)   Excuse me! (*To the others.*) Oh, this is hopeless.

Taylor   Louder.

Sainsbury (*calling*)   Hello there! Could I trouble you for a moment? (*To the others.*) What's his name?

Tate   Yes, what's his name? We don't know his name!

Sainsbury   Oh dear. This is really making bricks without straw. (*Calling*) Yoohoo . . . ! Listen, we all feel at one time or another that life isn't worth living. (*To the others.*) Is this right? Is this what one says?

Taylor   Keep going . . .

Sainsbury (*calling*)   I feel pretty terrible myself this morning.

Tate   I don't think he's listening.

Quine   He's going round the back of the chimneys.

They all give up.

Sainsbury   It doesn't work without the collar, you see.

Tate   You did your best, Dicky.

Sainsbury   I'm all right with sleeping pills. But I was away when they did ledges.

Headingley   Bad luck. Never mind. Off you all go.

He holds the door to the stairs open. **Snell** *enters. They all gasp.*

Snell   Yes! Me again!

They stare at him. They all swing round to look at the roof outside the window. Then back to look at **Snell**.

Thought you'd got rid of me, didn't you! And this time I'm not going until I've got some answers. Because it's one of you lot, I know.

Sainsbury (*joyously*)   I did it!

Snell   *You* did it?

Sainsbury   Me, yes! My goodness, I feel pleased with myself!

Snell   You! Of course!

Sainsbury   Oh, don't mention it. It's all part of the job.

Snell   Right.

He twists **Sainsbury**'s *arm behind his back.*

Sainsbury   What? What's happening?

Snell   If we don't find her I'm going to kick you to death.

He frogmarches **Sainsbury** *out of the room.*

Tate   He's taking hostages now!

Headingley (*urging the others out of the door*)   Stop him! Save him!

Tate *exits.*

Headingley (*to* **Quine**)   And your suit!

Quine   My suit, yes . . . !

Headingley   He's going to kill your suit!

He bundles **Quine** *out of the door.*

Headingley (*to* **Taylor**)   Get out there! Exert your authority!

Taylor   Have you got an aspirin?

Headingley   Bill Taylor! Bill Taylor's got an aspirin!

Taylor   I *am* Bill Taylor.

Headingley   *You're* Bill Taylor. Exactly!

Taylor   Aren't I?

Headingley (*propels* **Taylor** *towards the stairs door*)   So *you've* got an aspirin! (*Runs back to the window.*) Look! Look! They're walking on the grass!

Taylor *groans, and reluctantly allows himself to be shoved out of the door.* **Headingley** *runs to the bedroom door and flings it open.*

Headingley   Run!

The stairs door opens.

Wait!

He closes the bedroom door. Enter **Buckle** *from the stairs, very calm, with the flannel to his eye and a medical bag.*

Buckle   Always keep my little bag handy.

Headingley   Oh, it's you. David, David, David. Before anyone else comes in. Need your help.

Buckle (*extracts a hypodermic syringe and a phial*)   Yes – never know when someone may need a shot.

Headingley   No, listen. Listen, listen. Old friend. Yes? Trust you. Yes?

Buckle   Leave it to me, Chris. (*Tries to get the syringe into the phial, but keeps missing the target.*) Just wish I could see out of this eye.

Headingley   No, no, no. I've got a problem. Look!

He opens the bedroom door for a moment, while anxiously watching the staircase door, then closes it.

Buckle   What?

Headingley (*opens the door for a moment again*)   Look! Look! Look! (*Closes it.*) Yes?

Buckle (*baffled*)   No?

Headingley   Oh, come on, use your eyes! Use your eye!

He opens the door again, while still himself watching the staircase door. **Buckle** *peers into the bedroom out of his one good eye.*

Buckle   What am I looking at?

The staircase door opens, and **Headingley** *slams the bedroom door shut.*

Headingley   Nothing!

Enter **Snell** *from the stairs, still holding* **Sainsbury**, *with* **Tate**, **Quine**, *and* **Taylor** *attempting to separate them.*

Headingley Him!

Buckle (*to* **Snell**) Ah, there you are. Now come on, old chap . . . Hold him still, will you?

They try to.

Now, this won't hurt. Just a little prick.

Sainsbury Not me! Not me! Get that thing away from me!

Buckle That's you, is it? Which is him, then . . . ?

Quine Oh, get on with it!

Buckle Bit difficult to see.

Tate Have a go, anyway!

Buckle Right, here we come . . .

He jabs blindly at the moving mass of bodies.

Tate Ow!

Buckle Who was that?

Tate Me! Norman!

Buckle Don't worry. I didn't get much in.

Taylor Try again.

Buckle *jabs again.*

Taylor Ow!

Buckle Still wrong?

Taylor Yes!

Buckle Really need two eyes for this . . .

Quine Oh, for God's sake! Give me that thing!

He grabs the hypodermic and rams it into **Snell**, *who screams.*

Tate Bingo!

Taylor   We've got him!

Headingley   Right. Good. Fine. Well done. Now get him out of here.

He holds the staircase door open.

Buckle   All he needs now is a nice quiet lie down somewhere while the drug takes effect.

Headingley (*urging them out*)   Somewhere he can't do himself any harm.

Buckle   Two minutes, and he'll be as right as rain.

Headingley   Somewhere you can turn the key on him.

Tate   Good thinking, Chris.

He opens the bedroom door.

Headingley   No!

Quine   In you go.

Snell   I'll kick you to pieces!

Quine   Why not? Kick the whole room to pieces.

Sainsbury   Get it off your chest.

Headingley   No! No!

Snell   I'm a Fifth Dan!

Taylor   Good. You can practise in here.

*They force **Snell** into the bedroom while **Headingley** flails ineffectually at them to prevent them.*

Headingley (*beside himself*)   No! No, no, no, no, no, no!

Quine *takes the key from inside and locks the door.*

Headingley   Get him out of there!

Buckle   Get him *out* of there?

Headingley   Give me the key!

Taylor He's as mad as the other one!

They struggle to restrain him.

Headingley Take your hands off me! Everyone leave the room! That is an order! That is a directive issued by a Minister of the Crown!

Buckle Chris, what are you on about?

Headingley I can't explain! I refuse to explain! Listen! Listen!

They listen. Thumps, cries, crashes.

He's committing God knows what crimes in there!

Buckle He's just working off his feelings on the furniture.

Tate He won't come to any harm.

Headingley This must be stopped here and now!

Buckle If you're worried about him, let's take a look.

Headingley Don't go in . . . !

Buckle *Don't* go in?

Headingley Yes, get him out! No . . . ! But supposing . . . ? Oh my God! My whole scale of priorities is in question!

Sainsbury I've never seen anyone in such a state!

Tate You'd better give *him* a shot, David.

Buckle *goes to get his medical bag.*

Headingley Listen!

They listen. Silence.

(*Appalled.*) Silence!

Buckle I told you he'd quieten down.

Headingley He's done something terrible to her!

Sainsbury Her?

The penny drops.

Quine   Oh.

Buckle   Ah.

Tate   There *was* a lady in there?

Headingley   There was. There *is*. There was.

They are all suddenly sobered.

Buckle (*quietly*)   Unlock the door, Alan.

Quine *unlocks the door. Pause. The door opens. Pause.* **Snell** *emerges, now quiet and euphoric. They all stare at him.*

Headingley (*in a terrible voice*)   Where is she?

Snell *holds out* **Lady Driver***'s shoes. They all stare at them.*

Headingley   Her shoes!

He snatches them. **Snell** *holds out* **Lady Driver***'s bag.*

Headingley   Her bag! (*He snatches it.*) You've murdered her!

He rushes into the bedroom.

They gaze at **Snell** *in horror.*

Snell   I'm going out to buy a brocade waistcoat. For the wedding.

Tate (*quietly*)   I *knew* there was someone in there. I said! Didn't I, David? I'm not going in there, I said! I don't want to cause any red faces . . .

Headingley *comes out of the bedroom, the bag on his arm, holding the shoes and the sheet.*

Headingley   Her sheet!

Sainsbury   Her *sheet*?

Headingley   When last seen she was wearing this sheet.

They are all horrified.

Tate   Oh great creeping crocodiles!

Headingley *throws down the sheet and shoes and advances on* **Snell**.

Headingley   Her body! Where have you hidden it? Where? Where? Where?

Snell   In the chapel.

Headingley   In the *chapel*?

They all turn to look towards the window, then back at **Snell**.

Snell   With organ and choir. Reception in the Fellows' Garden. Weather permitting.

Headingley   Go to the Porter's Lodge, Norman. Ask Mr Birkett to call the police.

Tate *goes to the stairs door and opens it.* **Lady Driver** *enters, wearing her ordinary clothes, but no spectacles.*

Lady Driver (*stops in suprise at the sight of everyone*)   Oh . . .

Tate (*to* **Lady Driver**)   Something dreadful has happened.

He takes the bag off **Headingley**'s *shoulder and shows it to* **Lady Driver**.

Lady Driver   Ah! (*She goes to take the bag.*)

Tate   Someone's been murdered.

Lady Driver *stays her hand, shocked.*

Tate   A lady.

Quine   A girl.

Buckle   An old friend of Christopher's.

Tate (*hands the bag back to* **Headingley**)   Chris was just telling us all.

Headingley (*oblivious*)   This will of course destroy my career. It may also destroy the Government. It may even destroy the economy. But in the last few moments I have had to think, and to think deeply, about what I most value and what principles I hold most dear. And I know that if I attempted to conceal any knowledge that I have of this terrible thing . . .

He becomes aware of **Lady Driver**.

Headingley   Of this terrible . . . this terrible . . .

He looks at the bedroom. He looks at the bag. He looks at **Lady Driver** *again.*

Headingley   . . . this terrible . . .

Lady Driver   I seem to have interrupted his train of thought.

Tate   Yes, the police. I was fetching the police.

Headingley   One moment!

Tate *stops.* **Headingley** *sits down and covers his face with his hands. The bag slips on to his arm. They all look at him.*

Buckle   What is it, Chris?

Headingley (*takes his hands away from his face*)   We have a tradition in the House of Commons. A Member may rise and make a personal statement. (*He rises.*) He may say, in all sincerity and in all humility, 'I have made a mistake.' It is the practice on these occasions that the Member cannot be questioned on his statement. I believe that tradition is a fine and valuable one.

Quine   What?

Headingley   Today I stand not before the House but before my friends. And I say to you, as I would to the House, in all sincerity, and in all humility, 'I have made a mistake.'

Sainsbury   You mean . . . no one's been murdered?

Headingley (*humbly*)   I have made a mistake.

Tate   She's still there?

Headingley   I have made a mistake.

Quine   She never was there?

Headingley (*irritated*)   I have made a mistake!

Sainsbury   Oh.

Buckle   Well.

Tate   We all make mistakes.

Sainsbury   Very easy to do.

Tate   Poor old Chris.

Quine   Poor old Chris.

Taylor (*puzzled*)   Hold on. So this bag . . . ?

Pause.

Headingley (*makes the sacrifice*)   Is mine.

Taylor   Yours?

Buckle (*picks up the shoes*)   And these shoes?

Headingley   Mine.

Sainsbury   Well, you could knock me down with a feather boa!

Buckle (*hands **Headingley** the shoes, embarrassed*)   We all understand, Chris. We've all got our little secrets. (*Squeezes **Headingley**'s shoulder sympathetically.*)

Birkett *enters.*

Birkett   There's an ambulance outside waiting to take someone to hospital.

Lady Driver (*indicates **Headingley***)   This gentleman, I think, Mr Birkett.

Buckle (*indicates **Snell***)   Our friend here. (*To **Headingley**.*) Unless you want to come along, too, Chris, for a bit of a check up?

Headingley *shakes his head.*

Birkett   Oh, and a gentleman's suit.

*He holds up **Quine**'s suit, wet. **Quine** hobbles across to take it.*

Birkett   In the river, I'm afraid, Mr Quine, sir.

Quine (*to* **Headingley**)   You bastard!

Tate   Leave him be, Alan. Put our little differences behind us. Given the circumstances. (*Indicates the shoes and bag.*) Well, I suppose all good things must come to an end.

Sainsbury   Oh, is it over? Are we going?

Taylor   Not some of us. Some of us have still got the rest of our sentence to serve.

He exits.

Tate (*to* **Lady Driver**, *shaking hands*)   Norman Tate. The last time I saw you was playing Ophelia in fishnet stockings and black lace underwear.

Lady Driver   Oh yes. How nice to be remembered.

Tate   You wouldn't believe what's been going on in this old College of yours!

Lady Driver   As long as you all enjoyed yourselves.

Quine *begins to hobble off, still slightly bent over.*

Birkett   Brace up, Mr Quine, sir! We're not old gentlemen yet!

Quine   Twenty-five years older than we were yesterday, some of us. (*To* **Lady Driver**.) I suspect we have a lot to thank *you* for in keeping us entertained.

Lady Driver   The Master's wife is expected to make some contribution to the College's social life.

Quine (*referring to the suit*)   And even a little going-home present. Pneumonia.

Sainsbury (*feels his collarlessness*)   At least you've got something to wear. I feel quite *naked* . . . (*To* **Lady Driver**.) Unlike *you*, the last time I saw you!

Lady Driver   I'm relieved to hear it.

Sainsbury   You had a bunch of grapes and two walnut shells. (*To* **Headingley**, *discreetly, indicating the shoes and the bag.*)

Chris, I'll send you a little pamphlet that you may find helpful in coming to terms with things.

Headingley *nods.* **Sainsbury** *and* **Quine** *exit.*

Tate   Goodbye, then, Mr Birkett. A jolly super party. Thank you for having us.

Birkett   See you again in another twenty-five years, Mr Tate, sir.

Tate (*to* **Headingley**)   I'll be in touch, Chris. (*Indicates the shoes and the bag.*) We could do a rather tasteful little personal piece about it together before anyone else gets hold of the story.

Headingley *nods again.* **Tate** *exits.*

Buckle   Goodbye, then, Chris. Nice to catch up. Find out what you're up to these days.

Birkett   That eye, Mr Buckle, sir! Beefsteak on it as soon as you get home!

Buckle (*to* **Snell**)   Come on, then, old fellow. You and I are going to have a little ride in an ambulance.

Snell (*to* **Lady Driver**)   Formal, do you think? Bridesmaids? Morning suits?

Lady Driver (*smoothes her dress*)   There's a lot to be said for being in the right clothes.

Birkett (*to* **Snell**)   Goodbye, sir. Come and see us again. We shan't forget you next time!

Snell   I'll notify everyone of the date.

Buckle (*aside, to* **Birkett**, *as they leave*)   What's his name . . . ?

Lady Driver *and* **Headingley** *are left alone together.* **Headingley** *is still holding* **Lady Driver**'s *shoes and bag. He begins to bend down very slowly and cautiously to pick up the shaving foam, but can't make it.* **Lady Driver** *picks it up for him.*

Headingley   Thank you, Rosemary.

Lady Driver   Thank *you*, Christopher. (*She gently takes the shoes and the bag from him.*) You may be a fool, but at least you're a gentleman. (*She opens the bag and puts the shoes in.*) We must have that drink together.

Headingley   Look forward to it.

Lady Driver *finds inside the bag the letter she wrote to Roddy. She takes it out and looks at it. Then she crumples it up decisively.*

Lady Driver   Next time.

Headingley   Next time.

Exit **Lady Driver**.

Headingley *at last bestirs himself to action, and thoughtfully sprays shaving foam into his armpit as the curtain falls.*